PROLOGUE

This book is based on the biography of a woman, born and raised in a small town in Minnesota, who had the drive and ambition to fulfill her dreams. Paulyn Hofelman Laffrenzen had lived a relatively sheltered early life in Pipestone, Minnesota. Polly had a knack for turning even the most boring situations into adventures filled with excitement. She had a restless spirit that could not remain contained for too long.

Polly was a beautiful woman who radiated class, self-confidence, intelligence, and a fun-loving spirit. She was quite attracted to men, and as you will read in her story, they were very much attracted to her.

When she graduated from high school, Polly moved to Minneapolis. This was the beginning of her physically and emotionally tumultuous life. While attending college she held three jobs. She had a dream and a passion for life that would forever remain undaunted despite the many hardships, fears, and disillusions she would face throughout her life. Polly's search for fulfillment led her to travel to many cities, both in the United States and abroad.

Polly had a kind, caring, trusting heart. Unfortunately, it was because of this characteristic that Polly became the victim of a brutal rape, a disastrous marriage, and many heartbreaking relationships with men.

However, Polly's magnetic personality and fun-loving spirit were also the characteristics that won her many friends – female as well as male. In fact, her best friend Peggy was instrumental in Polly's success. She encouraged her, advised her, and at the lowest point of Polly's life, even saved her.

As you read the life and times of the Queen of Motel Boulevard, you will experience tears, heartache, laughter, and above all, the feeling that anything is possible if you want it bad enough and are willing to persevere as Paulyn Hofelman Laffrenzen did.

Polly dedicates this story of her life to:

Her son, Larry,
and daughters Pattie and Judy…

And to her departed son, Tommie.

Acknowledgements -

I am deeply grateful to my best friend, Peggy Sundahl, for being there for me in bad times and good times because without her friendship I might not be alive today.

I would also like to thank the Super 8 Motel Corporation, for giving me the opportunity to work for them. Ron Rivot and Dennis Brown were the finest bosses I have ever known.

I would also like to thank Emily Ann, Kenwood Gliberson, and Jay Ellingson.

Polly Hofelman Laffrenzen

CHAPTER 1

The Minnesota winters were as horrid as any winters of the Northern Plains. Wind gusts of up to seventy miles per hour and wind chill factors of fifty below zero made it impossible to fathom how human life could exist under such extreme conditions. The Indians survived the cold winters out of sheer determination. Before any white men ever came to this part of the country, the land was sacred to the Indians. The open meadows where the buffalo roamed were delightful. To the Indians the earth was their mother, and they loved and respected her. They were in total harmony with Mother Earth.

Family unity was the most important ingredient in their existence. Indian children were nurtured and never abused. Families loved their children more than the earth itself. A child was a gift from the Star God high in the heavens. He was never left unattended. This unique bond was a treasure to behold.

Hunting was the Indian way of providing food for the entire tribe. The meats were salted and hung out to dry. Jerky never spoiled and was quite nutritional.

The women gathered wild berries and natural herbs that were used by medicine men to cure ailments. Buffalo hides were used for winter clothing and throw rugs.

Summers were the most memorable times for the tribes because they were able to move from place to place. Camping next to a mountain stream was very important. The children played in the open meadows. They could also swim and catch fish for supper. At night, large campfires were built to keep warm because the nights got chilly. Families huddled around the campfire, and as the children listened intently, the Chief Elder would tell stories about the past. He related the same stories he had heard as a child. These stories were handed down from generation to generation. Some of them were intended to frighten the children in an effort to keep them from misbehaving. As a result, most of the children were very well-behaved.

The Sioux Indians who lived in the western part of Minnesota moved to an area where there was a waterfall and a picture-perfect lake. There were three rocks that the Indians called the Three Maidens. The Indians believed that these rocks possessed magical powers. The area where the three rocks was located was believed to possess special powers. It was such a strong belief amongst the Indians that they would walk over a thousand miles in search of the sacred red stone so they could carve out their peace pipes and smoke to the Great Spirit.

There was a time when many Indians died near the sacred quarry. Legend has it that Indians from many tribes had a major confrontation, and the blood of many warriors flowed like a river into fissures and cracks, turning the rocks red when the battle was over.

A beautiful white Indian maiden appeared as a ghostly image to two young warriors who were near death, showed them the red stone peace pipe, and said, "This is the covenant of our people. Smoke this on behalf of our people and never do battle on these sacred rocks again. Smoke the special blend of herbs and bark that I will give you to our Great Spirit in the heavens." She told them the blend they were to smoke was Kinnickinnick. She laid the peace pipe and a beaded leather pouch on the bloodstained rocks, where she ascended skyward.

The warriors lay there dumbstruck, not believing what they had just witnessed. They pinched themselves to make sure they were still alive. Suddenly a surge of energy consumed their almost lifeless bodies. They got up and walked over to the peace pipe and picked it up, feeling a magical power emanating from the pipe. They took the special blend of tobacco out of the pouch and filled the peace pipe. Using flint rocks, they built a small fire so that they could light the pipe, and began smoking. The smoke began to rise towards the heavens, and at that instant, they swore never to do battle on that sacred ground again.

The land around the quarry was scenic. There were various shrubs, bushes, trees, wildflowers, and cacti. The sight was breathtaking. The Indians decided to make this their home during the summer months. They dug for the precious stone so they could carve their sacred peace pipe. When the first peace pipe was carved it was considered to be a gift from the gods. The bowl was the altar, and the tobacco the sacred offering. The smoke carried messages to the gods.

Eventually, European explorers discovered the sacred region. The Indians shared the peace pipe with

French explorers as a token of friendship. It didn't take long for the rumors to spread amongst the Indian nations that the red stone pipe was quickly becoming the peace pipe of choice by the various Indian tribes. Red stone pipes were a viable representation of their ethnicity as red men. The pipe became their bible.

Red stone was relatively soft and easy to carve. French explorers named the pipe "Calumet", which means peace pipe. For each tribal family the pipe became a piece of memorabilia that was handed down from generation to generation.

CHAPTER 2

When a young Sioux Indian boy named Nikita entered the vision pit to seek the vision to achieve manhood, he brought his sacred pipe given to him by a medicine man. He spent four days in the pit alone and miles away from other humans. He was very frightened. He shivered because his naked body had only a thin blanket wrapped around it. He waited in anticipation for the Great Spirit to enter his soul and give him the vision and power he needed to become a man.

On the third day, the vision appeared and scared him terribly. His first impulse was to run, but he knew that if he ran he would never become a man. So he stayed. The apparition loomed around the pit. He could feel its power, which was so strong that he fell into a deep comatose state. He felt himself soaring with an eagle over the mountains and through the valley. Where the vision was taking him, he didn't know. On the fourth day his voice changed. His voice was rough, as if he had a frog in his throat.

In a matter of just a few days, Nikita had made the transformation from boyhood to manhood. When the medicine man came to take him out of the vision pit and off the mountain where he'd been for four days, he felt relieved. The vision he had just experienced gave him great trepidation. He was naïve, and had no idea what the outcome of his experience would be.

The medicine man wanted to know if Nikita had had a vision. One look at the expression on Nikita's face satisfied the medicine man. Nikita was cold, hungry and tired. Now he knew he had to be brave. He wanted to be a medicine man. He felt it was his destiny. As a medicine man he would be able to heal people just as his Sioux ancestors had done for many generations. As Nikita walked down off the mountain exhausted, he just wanted to sleep. As he walked, his body no longer belonged to him, but to a higher power. Only the medicine man could interpret the future outcome.

When Nikita arrived home he was met with cheers from the entire tribe. A great celebration would be held within a few days in honor of his becoming a man.

Nikita looked out at the crowd. He was searching for the girl he had been in love with since he was a young boy. He was now sixteen and had come into his manhood. At sixteen, he stood five feet ten inches tall with waist length black hair and high cheek bones that accentuated his handsome face.

Winonha was the young woman who had captured his heart. She had long jet-black hair that grew past her waist. Hers was the face of an angel. They were both certain that their destiny was to become husband and wife. Nikita knew that Winonha belonged to him and he would give his life for her. For many nights in the past he had had magical dreams about their future life together, and he longed for the day when his dreams would become a reality.

As he stood looking into the crowd, he knew the first thing he had to do was get some sleep. He waved at everyone and humbly thanked them. He walked towards the teepee as people cheered him on. This was his day! Upon entering the teepee he saw the many buffalo rugs strewn on the floor. He lay down and slept for two days. When he awoke, he ate ravenously. When he was through eating he went to the lake and bathed. The water against his body felt invigorating. He swam till he was tired. The other children watched with envy. The younger boys wanted to be just like him. His muscular build made him even more handsome.

Winonha walked out from behind some trees where she had been watching Nikita swim. Her heart was pounding so fast that she thought it was going to leap right out of her body. Nikita and Winonha stood gazing into each other's eyes. Winonha said, "It's so wonderful to see you, Nikita." He acknowledged the sentiment with a smile. His heart was racing as he felt Winonha's nearness. He had always been very quiet and shy but he managed to ask her if she would care to take a ride in the canoe. Eagerly she replied, "Yes, please. I would love to." They walked to the canoe, which was just a few feet away. It was constructed of rawhide fastened to wood. Winonha got into the canoe and Nikita pushed it into deeper water. He climbed in, picked up the oar, and slowly paddled towards the middle of the lake.

It was a beautiful summer day. Winonha watched as Nikita rhythmically paddled. The splashing water touching the sides of the canoe sounded like a drum beat. The canoe glided through wave after wave until it reached the other side of the lake, where Nikita and Winonha disembarked and walked toward several large rocks and tall ponderosa trees located just a few feet from the shore. It was a perfect spot for two people as madly in love as Nikita and Winonha. At a very early age, they knew they were destined to be together.

They sat on a grassy meadow near the rocks. There was something about these rocks that seemed to intensify the energy that was flowing through their bodies. Nikita took Winonha's hand and said, "When twelve moons have come and gone, I want to marry you. I will ask your parents for your hand in marriage. I have waited many moons for you, my love. It is time for you and I to share the same teepee and make children of our own."

A tear rolled down Winonha's cheek as she responded, "Oh yes, Nikita, I will marry you. I want to have your children." They gazed into each other's eyes for a moment, embraced, and shared a tender kiss. They were both virgins, and were willing to wait until they were married before consummating their love.

The following day a buffalo was slaughtered to commemorate Nikita becoming a man. As the celebration began, the women prepared a festive meal. Various gifts were given to Nikita by the different families of the tribe as a noble gesture in honor of his manhood.

Early on the morning of the celebration, Nikita was summoned by the tribal medicine man in order to more thoroughly interpret the vision Nikita had experienced while in the pit. He had to be completely truthful in relating what he had experienced. Nikita's vision most assuredly made him eligible to become a full-fledged medicine man. He would now become a student of ceremonial herbal medicine under the direct supervision of the Pejuta Wicasa. Gradually he would learn the Nagi way of the medicine man in order to help his people. He understood that he had a lot to learn but he had a burning determination to be the best medicine man he could be.

This was Nikita's most gratifying moment. Everything was perfect. He couldn't remember another moment as wonderful and memorable as the one he was now experiencing. The joyous laughter during the festivities in his honor was exactly as he had once envisioned it. The Great Spirit had spoken to him that night during his isolation in the pit. He felt so much closer to his mother, the Earth.

CHAPTER 3

Winonha became his universal partner when they married a year later. Nikita was ecstatic with his new bride by his side. Winonha was every bit the woman he had anticipated. Together they searched for the herbal medicine he needed to help cure the various diseases that befell his people. He smoked the yellow bark from the tree to give thanks to the Great Spirit. He held the peace pipe high above his head and spoke the words, "I pledge to you, Great Spirit, that if you guide me in the right direction I will not fail you or my people. Oh please, Great One, give me the strength and the power to do your work." He then ate *uncela* so he could better understand what his real purpose was in life. The peyote opened his mind. The visions he experienced under its influence were incredible. He saw the universe with such clarity that he was certain it was a great omen. At that moment, he knew he would never die. There was a higher purpose in life for him. His body was the vessel that contained his spirit, and his spirit was destined to eternal life.

Still under the influence, he had a vision that a pale-faced man would bring grave danger to his people. He envisioned the pale face coming from a land far away, and this confused Nikita. It didn't make any sense that people were coming to harm them. He told the medicine man of his vision. The medicine man told Nikita he had experienced the same vision. He said that the land that now belonged to them would be taken away from them. The devastation that would befall the Indian Nations saddened Nikita, and tears filled his eyes. Many of his people would perish at the hands of the pale face. Men, women, and children, young and old, would die. He spoke to Winonha about his vision, and they both cried bitterly. Winonha didn't understand why their god would allow these atrocities.

Life went on for this small tribe. They handcrafted the red stone pipes. Before any stones were ever carved, they went through a special ritual giving thanks to the Great Spirit. Selling the peace pipe was a way to make a living. They bartered for anything of value. The work was tedious. Working the quarries was hard work, but for years this had been their custom. It was in their blood. They fashioned some of the most beautiful ceremonial peace pipes in the world. Chiefs from many different Indian nations traveled a great distance to purchase the red stone peace pipe.

There was talk that the white man was making his push for land that belonged to the Indians, and that wars would come because of the white man. Death and destruction were inevitable.

A year to the date that Nikita and Winonha were married, a vibrant young son came into their world. They named him Little Wolf. He was as handsome as his father. He had the darkest of eyes and his mother's jet-black hair. He was a bundle of joy. It made Nikita a very proud father. He stared at the child for hours. He could not believe that he had a son. His life was now complete. He loved Winonha more than ever.

CHAPTER 4

White settlers came in droves to Minnesota and settled on the barren plains. They built their towns and cities. As immigrants began to move into the new territory, the Indian nations began to lose ground. Nikita and his people were distraught because life as they once knew it would never be the same. Ironically, the solid footing the Indians once possessed across America was now trampled under statehood. The Indians were moved to reservations. The great buffalo hunts the Indians once cherished vanished along with their freedom. Nikita and his people were very fortunate that the white man didn't much care about their part of the country because of its isolation. Most of the white people headed for the high country, the Colorado Rockies.

The Gold Rush was on. Multitudes of gold-crazed men came west to get rich at any cost, even murder. Gold fever was in the air and there was no stopping it. The part of Minnesota where Nikita and his tribe lived was safe from the Gold Rush. Most white settlers stayed away because it was Indian country. The

Indians lived in their own little world away from all the madness as they continued to carve their red stone peace pipes.

In September 1873, a man by the name of C. H. Bennett visited the area after reading a poem written by Henry Wadsworth Longfellow. Longfellow had written a well-known poem entitled "Song of Hiawatha". Bennett fell in love with this part of the country. The following April, Daniel E. Sweet surveyed a twenty-block town site. The site chosen was a mile south of the Pipestone quarries. The first pine shanty was built by Bennett but he never lived in it. Mr. and Mrs. Sweet, their son Henry, and a man named John Lowry moved into the Bennett shanty the same day it was built, establishing the first temporary home in the area. In August 1874, the Sweet family moved into the first permanent home erected.

It wasn't long before Pipestone became a town and the surrounding land was being purchased at six dollars per acre. The area began to grow rapidly. Settlers came from all parts of the country. Pipestone experienced considerable growth. By June 1879 many businesses and three physicians were open for business. The boom was on. Mr. Bennett had become an avid promoter of Pipestone. The town and the county were named after the red stone used to make the peace pipe.

The Sioux quarry site had large deposits of the stone that was used to construct the first building in Pipestone. Masons, builders, and quarry men came from all parts of the country to begin the intricate process of constructing stone buildings. The craftsmen were some of the best in the New World. The quarry men cut each stone with great precision, and the masons started putting the stone buildings together. The work was hard and the days were long. It took a lot of manpower and energy. The architectural designs of the buildings and the craftsmanship were of the highest quality.

The Sioux quartzite buildings had a special beauty because of the way the stone was cut and arranged. The joints were marked, and the masons used rough-faced stone. They used a large variety of different-sized blocks to face the buildings. Multicolored stones were used from the different quarries to give contrast to the buildings.

The Pipestone development was a sight to behold. All of the buildings being constructed on Main Street were an ostentatious expression of the magnificent craftsmanship which made Pipestone the most unique town in western Minnesota. These buildings were constructed by men who took great pride in their craft.

Mr. Bennett, who came from Lemars, Iowa, was a druggist. He operated the local drug store. His wife promoted cultural activities. One of the most important historical dates for Pipestone City was Thanksgiving Day 1879 because it was on that day that the first train arrived in Pipestone. Pipestone soon became a major railroad center, with four lines into the city.

In 1891, Congress passed a bill that appropriated $30,000 to build the Pipestone Indian Training School approximately a mile north of town on the reservation. The purpose of its construction was to educate the Indian children living on the reservation.

In the 1880's a man named August Johnson moved to Pipestone from Sweden. Mr. Johnson and his wife Augusta purchased the second rock quarry next to the Sioux quarry near the reservation. They also purchased farmland nearby. They built their own home on the three hundred acres. Mr. Johnson was a very hard worker. Independent contractors worked the quarry fields to extract the hard stone. As new buildings were being erected in Pipestone, all the material was being used up by masons.

The rapid growth of Pipestone was astonishing. Olive Street was starting to look more like a town every day. Pioneers continued coming to Pipestone from all parts of the country. What was appealing to the settlers was how handsome the buildings were, and the fact that they could use the stone to build.

Mr. Leon H. Moore, an artist, constructed the Moore block. The building's most unique feature were the sandstone sculptures, which sometimes were called gargoyles. The gargoyles were molded, not carved. It was a method Moore had learned while in art school. One of Moore's masterpieces was the face of Moses. A high level of craftsmanship went into his buildings, and he was commended for his outstanding designs. He constructed a few other buildings and became highly respected in the community. Moore was a man of many talents.

CHAPTER 5

The sixty-room Calumet Hotel was built of wood with veneered brick in 1883 at a cost of $25,000. It was the pride of Pipestone. On December 15, 1886, in temperatures twenty-five degrees below zero, a fire destroyed the hotel in just two hours after it literally exploded. The town had no firefighting equipment. A Baptist minister lost his life and others were injured in the blaze. In a matter of two hours, the pride of Pipestone was nothing but a heap of ashes. Although the landowner considered rebuilding, and townspeople contributed several thousand dollars to rebuild the hotel, he decided to invest his money elsewhere.

A couple of bankers from the Bank of Southwestern Minnesota announced that their intention to rebuild the hotel with all the conveniences it once had. The added attraction would be a first-class bank to accommodate the townspeople in their financial needs. The new hotel would be built on land at the corner of Hiawatha Avenue and Olive Street, which the bankers had purchased at an estate sale. The hotel was very important to the economy of Pipestone because the town had four railroad lines, and it needed a place to house all the traveling salesmen who were coming into the territory.

Two different types of quartzite were used to build the new Calumet Hotel, red Sioux quartzite, and pink jasper quartzite. Construction began in the spring of 1888 and was completed on November 1st. The pride of Pipestone was back. A Grand Opening celebration was held on Thanksgiving Day. The hotel was fire-proof.

Pipestone City was still growing at a rapid pace. It was being landscaped with trees and flowers. Signs of a beautiful town were in the making. A large portion of the homesteaders were people of good moral character - teachers, doctors, lawyers, stone cutters, tradesmen, and farmers. Some of the first homesteaders who settled around Pipestone City before its development were Civil War veterans. They had "script" which gave them military recognition for their service and entitled them to a quarter section of land where they had to erect a building and till the soil.

Most of the Civil War veterans were eager to get their lives on the right track after the war. The transition from military to civilian life was not easy. Thus, working the soil gave these veterans the opportunity to make a new beginning. Wealthy investors coming from England invested money to buy land, and at the request of Mr. Bennett, built up Pipestone. It was a very prodigious effort by Mr. Bennett. He was proud of Pipestone City.

The Close brothers helped this small but thriving community grow immensely, and they made generous deals with the farmers in an effort to help them build a house, a barn, and acquire a team of horses and a wagon. These brothers did everything they could to help the farmers get started, and the farmers didn't have to pay any money back for a period of ten years. They bought up land for schools as well as railroad land. The Close brothers helped in every way they could; money was not an obstacle for them. They had accumulated large holdings.

Even with the town in full ascendancy, the people of Pipestone were kind, generous, and humble. They were dedicated to the preservation of the most unique town in Minnesota. The sacred quarries caught the attention of the explorers and settlers alike. They came in great numbers to immerse themselves in the indefinable vibes that emanated from the sacred red stone, which had a powerful magnetism unknown to people who didn't understand the way of the Indian. The magical mystery was the driving force behind this universal power. We will never understand their simple adherence to it because we, as human beings, have a tendency to be skeptical about things we don't understand.

We must remember that we are one with the universe. To deviate from that would break the number one commandment of the universe. We are forever intertwined as one. The Indians understood the spiritual significance of this basic law. They lived it and taught it to their children. They never disturbed the most important element of their existence, Mother Nature.

The City Fathers of Pipestone City established a fair and friendly relationship with the Indians. Even though the Indians were already living on the reservation, coexistence was a goal the City Fathers aspired to. As the city continued to expand and thrive, walkways were built and streets were maintained on a regular basis. Trees were planted, as were wildflowers and wild cactus, in an effort to enhance and add character to the city.

At the turn of the century, when the automobile came to Pipestone, things began to change. The railroad began to be replaced by trucks, which were used to transport goods and commodities, making life a lot easier for everyone living in the Plains states. Farmland was bought up by settlers and buckboards and wagons became obsolete. Farm life went through a dramatic transition period. Steam-driven tractors were now plowing the fields, replacing plow horses. This agricultural phenomenon began to take place across America.

Buffalo no longer populated the land. Black Angus cattle were purchased and transported to the area. Cattle became part of the landscape. When early Spanish conquistadors came to the New World, they brought horses and cattle with them. Spaniards introduced many important things to America during the exploration of this country which have become incorporated in our lives today.

During this period, machinery was becoming a very important part of people's lives. Progress and modernization had arrived. It was welcome, especially during the winter months, which were very harsh and brought with them some difficult times.

Some of the children had to travel a long way to school, either on foot or horseback. Many of the children attended school at the country schoolhouse during the 1880's. As the surrounding area grew, a new school was badly needed. Eventually, a school was built which had all the modern conveniences in contrast to the old country schoolhouse.

The majority of the immigrants moving to Pipestone City were Germans, Scandinavians, Scots, Irish, and English. Everyone brought a different talent from his particular country in Europe. The stonemasons deserve a great deal of credit for all the beautiful buildings they erected in Pipestone City.

A variety of businesses sprouted up all over the City, including as many as eight saloons that thrived because of the men who liked to indulge in the consumption of spirits. This was a way for them to socialize and relieve a little tension after a hard day's work. They would exchange tales from the past that were sprinkled with a touch of exaggeration. Boisterous laughter could be heard throughout the City as intoxicated men enjoyed each other's company late into the night.

A fracas would at times break out. These inebriated men would disagree about the most ludicrous things. The liquor made them feel brave and dulled their common sense, loosened their tongues, and resulted in foolish arguments for which they would suffer a great deal of remorse the following day along with massive hangovers. They would, however, repeat the ritual each day because they were lonely and in need of companionship.

With the automobile coming of age, roads had to be built, so Mr. Bennett set out to survey roads leading to the surrounding towns linking Pipestone to the rest of the world. It was the most important step the city had to take, and the City Fathers wanted to do a good job. Mud was something that made travel difficult during the winter months, and blowing snow on the plains was hellish. Snow drifts would at times be six to eight feet high, clogging the main arteries in and out of Pipestone. Supplies were delayed many times.

The brutality of the winter months was seldom welcome to the people of Pipestone. The winters in the northern plains were very long. Most of the farmers waited in anticipation for spring to return so they could plant their seeds – seeds that would yield enough food for the stock as well as for domestic use.

During the summer months, farmers worked under the most arduous conditions, fighting the elements and the grasshoppers in an effort to protect their corn, wheat, and all the other essential crops. It was not an easy task. The women would can many of the foods they cultivated. They built root cellars to store all the provisions. Living in No Man's Land was a hindrance, so people had to learn to be self-sufficient just to survive the long winter months. Another basic and crucial commodity was fuel. Some of the most commonly used fuels were wild grass, corncobs, wood, coal, and kerosene.

CHAPTER 6

The Johnson quarry north of town provided a great deal of the stone that was going into the buildings being constructed in Pipestone City. August Johnson and his family were doing so well they decided to get into the cattle business. They bought a few head of Black Angus cattle. Life was good to this European family who had come to America with the dream of making a living. All they wanted to do was acquire a piece of land and build a home. It was a dream that August Johnson had clung to ever since the first time he heard about the potential the New World had to offer. His dream had not only been fulfilled, but had far surpassed his expectations.

His children were his life, and he nurtured them as best he could through their adolescent years. Johnson's oldest daughter had just graduated from high school. Lillian was a sight to behold. She had long black wavy hair, the darkest brown eyes, a slender build, and a carefree personality. Her incessant smile was quite infectious and endearing. She was spunky and full of life. Lillian loved to dance, so on weekends she'd go dancing. Different families would sponsor a dance in their homes. They would clear all the furniture out of the living room and play records on the phonograph.

Ever since Lillian was young, she had had a crush on one particular boy named Art Hofelman. Art had blond hair and a somewhat serious demeanor. He had also, for the longest time, had the same feelings about Lillian. Whenever he saw her at the dances, his stomach would become queasy. He knew that sooner or later he would have to work up the nerve to ask the lovely Lillian to dance.

He stood in the midst of a crowded living room with kids his own age. A wave of shyness seemed to sweep the room. The phonograph blared, and toes began tapping to the rhythm. The kids were getting antsy and restless. They were ready to dance. As everyone surveyed the room for some sign of encouragement, a couple finally walked out onto the middle of floor and began to slow dance. Before long other couples followed their lead. With sweaty palms and racing hearts, couples soon filled the dancing area.

Art glanced across the room towards Lillian. They seemed to be the only couple not dancing. Art felt out of place, and decided to conquer his fear and ask her to dance. He walked up to Lillian and asked shyly, "May I please have this dance?" She said, "Yes." For the rest of the night they were inseparable. The opportunity they had longed for had finally presented itself. The ice had been broken and they were now together. They had found the perfect love. They had waited so long for this moment.

An incredible feeling swept through their bodies. It was a feeling neither one had ever experienced before. They held on to each other wishing this night would never end. This magic night marked the beginning of a new life for Art and Lillian.

Several months later, Art and Lillian were married in a simple wedding ceremony. The Hofelmans and Johnsons were very happy for their children. Art and Lillian were both very young but they knew they wanted to be together forever. They were very much in love.

Art was only fourteen when he had dropped out of school to seek employment at various ranches around Pipestone. Wherever he was employed he would ask the rancher if he could sleep in the barn. Art had left home at such an early age because his father, Henry, drank too much. Henry loved going to the saloons, getting drunk with his friends, and telling tall tales of yesteryear. Some of the tales had been in the family for many generations.

Art and his father didn't see eye to eye about a lot of things, so by mutual agreement, he decided to make it on his own. At first Art was despondent about the way things had turned out between him and his father but he knew it was the only way to avoid conflict. Now that he was on his own, he was lonely and homesick but it was a small price to pay for the serenity he had found being away from his father.

Sleeping in strange barns was not easy, and most nights he got very little sleep because of the freezing cold. He slept on a bed made of straw with only a thin Army blanket to keep him warm. He would stare at the rafters, and as dawn appeared on the horizon, he could see his breath. He missed the warmth of his home and his mother's home cooking. He remembered how, when he was younger, his life had been filled with joy and laughter. They were a happy family in those days. Unfortunately, his father's drinking had changed all that.

He despised his father for his drinking, which forced Art to live like a vagabond at the mercy of strangers. He was often exhausted from lack of sleep but he had to get up and get moving before hypothermia set in. As he did so, he wondered what breakfast would consist of that morning. He would quickly usher the cow into the barn and milk her. It was a good way to get something nutritious in his stomach. It would also warm him up.

For the first few years after he left home, life for Art was difficult – going from ranch to ranch and sleeping in barns. This was the life he had been forced to choose, and even though it appalled him, he had to accept it. His dreams and the hope of marrying the girl of his dreams were the only thing that kept him from giving up. He longed for the day that he would marry and have a family of his own. Because of his own chaotic childhood, he knew he would make every effort to give his children the love and security he'd never had.

Marrying Lillian brought an end to his nightmare. He would no longer be sleeping in barns with spiders, snakes, and rodents. Tonight he would be sleeping with his lovely new bride, whom he would cherish for the rest of his life. The night of the dance, for the first time in many years, Art had slept like a baby.

When Art and Lillian got married they were completely broke. They had no money, just lots of love. The intensity of their love for each other would bond them together. Nothing and no one could ever separate them because they firmly believed in their marriage vows, which they took very seriously. For them it was "Until death do us part". A few days after they were married, they moved into their new home, which they were allowed to rent because it had been repossessed by the government.

Art went back to work after their brief honeymoon. For the first time in his life he felt like a complete man. The love of his life, Lillian, played a big part in his newly found confidence. While working, he would daydream about Lillian and could scarcely wait till he could get home to her. Lillian stayed home and cleaned house, washed clothes, and cooked. She, in turn, could hardly concentrate on her housework because Art continually occupied her thoughts. Love was wonderful!

When Art got home at night, the newlyweds were so ecstatic at the sight of each other that they fell into each other's arms. They missed each other so much when they were apart that they were reluctant to end the embrace. Their love was unconditional.

As time went on, Lillian became pregnant. She was thrilled. When she imparted the good news to Art, he looked at her in disbelief. His face became flushed with excitement. He wanted a son, and by the grace of God, he prayed this little miracle would turn out to be a boy.

For the next few days, Art could think of nothing except the new life his wife was carrying. He found it very hard to keep his mind on his work. Little by little he became used to the idea that in the near future he would become a father. Nine months seemed like an eternity.

Finally, the time arrived and Lillian gave birth to a little boy whom they named Art Jr. He was a handsome lad and the spitting image of his father. Art and Lillian stared with awe at the little miracle they had brought into this world. Life was good!

The next day Art returned to work. He told all of his friends about the birth of his son, who was his pride and joy. All of his co-workers congratulated him.

When little Art Jr. turned five, Lillian gave birth to a baby girl. She had golden blonde hair and brown eyes. She, too, resembled her father. This little angel stole her father's heart. She became daddy's little girl. She was cute as a button. Art and Lillian named their little girl Paulyn. Her name fit perfectly as she was quite petite. The Hofelman family was now complete.

Both the Johnson and Hofelman grandparents were very proud of their grandchildren. Grandmother Johnson couldn't pronounce Paulyn so she started calling her Polly. Little Polly stole Grandmother Johnson's heart. Her grandmother loved her to death.

Grandmother Johnson lived across the street from her daughter Lillian, and visited the baby every day. Little Sonny, as he was also called, couldn't quite make out what all the fuss was about. All he knew was that he was no longer the baby. Polly was getting all of the attention. Once in a while he'd go to the baby's room and sneak a peak while she slept. He was astounded at how small her hands were. He also noticed her cute little nose. He thought to himself, Maybe I can get used to this. When she gets bigger we can probably play together.

At first he was very jealous of little Polly. He resented not being the baby anymore; but, after all, this was his little sister. The more he thought about it, the easier it was to get used to the idea that this baby was here to stay.

When Polly turned a year old, the economy began to falter. The Great Depression started to sweep across America like a deadly tornado, leaving people hungry and homeless in its wake. The stock market tumbled to its knees, leaving most Americans in financial disarray and putting the American dream temporarily on hold.

Many families around Pipestone were losing their ranches, and everything was being rationed with coupons and government stamps. These times were very lean for a lot of folks. Family unity was very essential for their mere survival. During these lean years, people planted huge gardens to supplement food shortages. They helped each other in any way they could.

The very first time someone drove the first car into Pipestone, many people were very skeptical. The general opinion was that there was no way in damnation that a car would ever replace the horse. It was just a new fad that would soon die out. These skeptics ended up eating their words. The automobile became the most important part of the Industrial Revolution. Everyone wanted to acquire one. The demand for automobiles was so great that there was no way to keep up with the demand.

Oil became an important part of our society. Machinery was being utilized by virtually everyone. Oil and gas demands skyrocketed. Supply and demand was greater than oil production. Consequently, the government had to begin rationing gasoline for automobiles by issuing coupons for this commodity. This didn't sit well with a lot of the ranchers. How were they going to cultivate the necessary quotas of wheat and corn? They were in a no-win situation.

When little Polly turned two years old, her daddy gave her a puppy. This made Polly very happy. The puppy jumped on Polly and started licking her face, which made her laugh with joy. From that day forward, Polly and her puppy were inseparable. They named the dog Sally. She was well behaved and became very protective of little Polly. When strangers came around the ranch, Sally would bark her head off until she was assured that everything was all right, whereby she would calm down. This was Sally's territory, and she chewed on the heels of strangers to let them know.

The Indian school was located down the street from the Hofelmans, and when the Indian kids walked past the Hofelman home Sally would raise a fuss.

CHAPTER 7

Many children from the different reservations around the country attended the Indian school. The Indian student population consisted of Sioux, Chippewa, Sac, Fox, Oneida, Pottawatomie, Omaha, Winnebago, Gros Ventre, Arickaree, and Mandan. The children ranged in age from 6 years old to 18 years old.

The persons responsible for the construction of the Indian school were Mr. and Mrs. Whitehead. Like everyone else at that time, they had heard about "The Song of Hiawatha". They decided to visit the sacred quarry in August 1873. While they were there, they filed on a piece of land they felt was appropriate for a school. Because Mr. Whitehead was a Civil War Veteran, he had script which gave him the authority to file on the land. He was a righteous man and respected for his religious beliefs by the many settlers who knew him.

He came to care a great deal about the Indians and was very sensitive to their needs. He wanted to do everything he could to help them. There was a rumor that the government wanted to build four Indian schools somewhere in the United States. Mr. Whitehead thought this was the perfect place to erect one of them. The Indians would need a boarding school because many of the children would have to come from distant reservations around the country.

In 1891 they constructed the first building using the stone from the Indian quarry. The initial building housed a few pupils to begin with, but attendance gradually grew. The pupils were furnished with the basic necessities such as food, clothing, medical supplies, transportation, and dental service. Because there wasn't enough money, the students had to perform many of the domestic duties such as cooking, washing, and baking. They also had to mend their own clothing. The students milked the cows, fed the animals, cultivated the garden, and maintained the grounds as well as the inside of the buildings.

Vocational and academic courses were taught in the school. The girls were schooled in domestic subjects that would enable them to maintain a household when they went out into the world.

As little Polly got older, she went to visit Grandmother Johnson almost every day. The Indian children used to frighten her, possibly because they were different. She really couldn't pinpoint what it was about these children that scared her. Every time the Indian children walked by, she would seek shelter behind something until they were gone. Her heart would be pounding so hard she thought it would leap right out of her chest. Even with Sally by her side to protect her, she was still uneasy.

Sally became her best friend. They were inseparable. Wherever Polly went, Sally tagged along. Sally was very intelligent and most obedient.

Polly loved spending her time at grandma's. Polly enjoyed the way grandma spoiled her as well as the fact that she had her grandmother wrapped around her little finger. Her grandmother allowed her to get away with murder, whereas her mother was not so indulgent. Polly's mother was a strict disciplinarian.

The year was now 1934. It was Polly's first day of school and she was afraid to leave her secure little world. The inquisitive stares from so many unfamiliar faces made her very uneasy, but Polly was headstrong and refused to be intimidated. She hid her fear well and returned stare for stare.

As she looked around the classroom, she was aghast at how huge it appeared. The blackboard occupied an entire wall of the classroom. Since Polly couldn't read as yet, the writing on the blackboard was foreign to her. As she became familiar with her surroundings, she began to relax. She sensed that the other children were just as nervous and scared as she was. She was sure they shared her desire to be home in familiar surroundings.

Sally, her dog, dominated Polly's thoughts. She missed her so much that the pain was almost unbearable. She could scarcely wait for school to be out so she could rush home to her precious little Sally.

At recess, Polly's best friend Marion clung to Polly's coat as they ran around the playground. Marion was quite a character and loads of fun to be with.

In class, Polly had to sit in one of the tall chairs because she had very long legs. Marion, on the other hand, had short legs but insisted on sitting in one of the tall chairs so she could be near Polly. It was hilarious the way Marion's short legs dangled from the chair. Just watching her made Polly crack up. They would look at each other and start giggling. The fact that there were so many unfamiliar faces in the classroom didn't bother Polly and Marion because they had each other. Kindergarten was the first step in learning how to interact with others, but these two friends were oblivious of anyone except each other.

Lillian made Polly wear a 3/4-length bright red coat and large red bow because she reasoned it would make Polly stand out and thus keep her from being run over. As it turned out, her attire became her personal trademark.

In the summer of 1934, on the Fourth of July, Pipestone held its annual parade. Sally had given birth to a litter of puppies so Lillian decided to dye Sally and her puppies pink. Sally was a Spitz, and the puppies were just as darling as their mother. Lillian decorated Polly's wagon, and when she was done she was quite pleased. She knew she would get a reaction from the community, but to what extent she did not know.

It was a perfect day with only a few clouds dotting the vivid blue sky. It was the kind of day that would bring out the curiosity seekers. Most of the people were dressed in casual wear. They lined the streets in anticipation of the parade which would travel down Main Street. People had begun lining both sides of the street. Polly and her dogs were attracting quite a bit of attention.

The parade finally got under way, to the cheers and joyous laughter of the crowd. Lillian pulled the wagon as little Polly sat proudly erect. The pretty red bow she wore on her hair was definitely an eye-catcher. Sally barked at the crowd and her puppies mimicked their mother. No one had ever seen pink dogs before, so naturally, all eyes were on Polly and her dogs. Polly waved at the crowd and they waved back at her. Someone in the crowd yelled "Hurrah!

Hurrah!" People began to clap as Polly and her dogs passed by.

Everyone seemed to be thoroughly enjoying himself. Pipestone was alive and the City Fathers were very proud. Their dream of building a town in this part of Minnesota had been fulfilled. It was a wonderful little community, and the buildings along Main Street were a beautiful sight to see. Pipestone had come of age, and the community was ready to participate in the twentieth century.

The Great Depression had stifled the economy in Pipestone, and no one in the nation had been spared its devastating effects. Many people were still suffering. The most difficult years were 1932 and 1933. Hunger had spread across America – famine does not discriminate. The larger cities had suffered most, and the children most of all. Poverty spread like gangrene. Even with the government food programs, food shortages were still enormous. Ranchers had the greatest advantage because they could grow their own gardens and obtain meat by killing a cow or a pig. Being self-sufficient had its advantages.

Things were getting better but there was a lot of healing still to be done. Following the parade, the citizens of Pipestone gathered at the local city park for a picnic so that the families of Pipestone could intermingle. Little Polly and her pink dogs were the talk of the town. The women especially thought they were adorable.

The following day, Lillian received several phone calls from various women around town who were interested in buying the pink puppies, and of course she had to tell everyone that she had dyed them for the parade. No matter, though, because they still thought the puppies were adorable.

As the school year progressed, Polly became acquainted with the other children. She and a lot of the other little girls became very close, and during recess they would chase the cute boys around the playground. But the boys were much faster, and their pursuit was futile. They did, however, give it their best shot. With their little faces as red as beets and sweaty, the girls stopped just long enough to catch their breath before they continued their chase. Off they would go trying to catch the little boy of their dreams. Polly knew at a very young age that she had a thing for boys. She was so boy crazy that for her the only good thing about school was the boys. She wanted a boyfriend for herself.

There was something about boys that brought out the best in Polly. Even at an early age it was quite evident that Polly didn't have a shy bone in her body. She was a free-spirited soul with a very outgoing personality. Polly was a lot like her father. Her mother, who was more conservative, made the care of her family her number one objective in life. She made sure her house was clean, the meals were prepared on time, and the clothes were washed and pressed. She nurtured her children and was a good wife, mother, and lover. Her life was totally fulfilled.

Polly's family had very little money, and the Depression made things more discouraging for everyone. The one bond that held the American people together was their faith in God. Without that strong faith, this country would have suffered a greater crisis.

Winters during the Depression were very difficult for a lot of the Northern Plains people. They made some incredible sacrifices just to squeeze by. Sometimes it would snow so much that it stranded people in their homes for days at a time. In order for them to get from one place to another, they had to tunnel their way around town. At night, when families huddled around the stoves to keep warm because of the sub-freezing temperatures, the powerful howling winds shook the walls of the houses. The windows looked like etched glass where condensation adhered to the windows, giving them a bottled effect. Most of the families slept in their living rooms because the rest of the house was much too cold.

There were few forms of entertainment. Some families had phonographs or radios. Many played instruments. Family unity was one of the most important elements in keeping a family together. Another form of entertainment was story telling. Families would share stories brought from the old country. The children loved to listen to these stories about relatives who still lived in Europe.

Polly had grown like a weed during summer vacation, so when she started the second grade she was a head taller than most of her classmates. Her ever-present colorful bow was still on her head and she wore her bright red coat. Marion was still Polly's best friend. Their new teacher was Ms. Jensen. Ms. Jensen was in her mid-thirties and had a slender figure, blonde shoulder length hair, dark blue eyes, and a jovial demeanor. She was the kind of teacher that made you pay attention.

Polly didn't much care for school. She was a daydreamer. Her current preoccupation was a boy named Lyle. She had fallen head over heels in love with little Lyle. She thought he was the cutest boy she had ever laid eyes on. It was just an infatuation, but for Polly it was true love, and she was determined to capture his heart. Lyle was totally oblivious of Polly's attempts to gain his attention. Having a girlfriend was, at this point, the furthest thing from his mind. Polly became obsessed with Lyle and would not be deterred in her efforts to gain his attention. She had no doubt that she could, and would, get him to fall madly in love with her.

On weekends, Polly would walk to her grandma's house with Sally at her side. Sally was such an intelligent dog that she stood between Polly's legs making sure the coast was clear before allowing her to cross the street. Grandmother was always very glad to see her favorite granddaughter. When Polly arrived, her grandmother would immediately fix her something to eat.

Polly's grandmother kept busy canning the produce she had grown in her garden. It took her a whole week to can everything. Sometimes she and Polly would go out to the barn to milk the cows. They also enjoyed taking long walks across the open meadows in the fresh autumn breeze. Polly cherished the time she spent with her grandmother because she loved her so very much. In her mind and heart she couldn't imagine how life could get any better. She and her grandmother always had so much fun together.

When they returned to the house, her grandmother would serve hot chocolate and cookies, after which Polly would take a short nap. During her nap she would dream of Lyle. In her dream, Lyle came to the realization that Polly was the girl of his dreams. He would realize what a fool he had been not to pursue Polly. He would eventually proclaim his love for her and they would develop a passionately romantic relationship. Just when Polly was in the throes of this dream, her dog's barking would rudely awaken her. She would rub her eyes and sit up in bed totally despondent that it had only been a dream.

Polly would call out to her grandmother, who startled by the urgency of her cry, came running and ask, "What's the matter, darling?" Polly would reply, "Oh, Granny, I was having the most wonderful dream when Sally's barking woke me up." Grandmother would sit on the edge of the bed and cradle Polly in her arms, and in her Swedish accent, assure her everything would be all right. Polly would lay her head against her grandmother's shoulder and close her eyes. She always felt much better after her grandmother's reassurance. Polly was certain that no matter what obstacles she encountered, her grandmother would always be there for her.

When the weekend was over and Polly returned home, her daddy was happy to see her because he missed his little girl. He sat rocking her on his favorite rocking chair. He listened as Polly told him all about her weekend at grandma's.

Polly was daddy's little girl and he catered to her every whim. Her brother Sonny was extremely jealous and resentful of the special relationship that Polly and her father shared. Sonny and Polly were never close.

Sonny was now twelve years old. He had reached the age of puberty and was responsible for doing the many chores around the house such as feeding and milking the cows, as well as feeding the chickens and rabbits. During the summer months he helped with weeding the garden, and during the winter he had to shovel the snow off the walkways, which was time-consuming because the snow was quite deep. All in all, Sonny was a very busy boy.

Polly often wondered why Sonny never paid attention to her. He was her big brother and she craved his attention. She loved him very much and couldn't understand why he never had time to play with her. Now that he was older, he had some pretty big shoes to fill because he wanted to be like his father.

In school he was quite popular and had a few girls chasing after him. He was still too shy to have a girlfriend. He and some of his buddies were, as yet, not brave enough to approach girls. When they got together they would discuss girls, especially the prettiest and most popular. At this stage in his life, his education was far more important than girls. Polly, on the other hand, was quite different. She was far more preoccupied with boys than schoolwork, so it was no surprise that her studies were far from satisfactory.

Polly was totally crazy about Lyle and she was quite persistent in pursuing him. She was determined to make him like her. Lyle, however, continued to rebuff her. Even though her feelings were hurt, she refused to show it. She decided that if Lyle didn't want anything to do with her, he could bloody well go to hell. She would find someone else. Lyle was not the only fish in the sea. It took her a while to get over the hurt of rejection, so in the meantime, she stayed within her circle of girlfriends because she found boys far too complicated.

When Polly was in the fourth grade, part of her school burned down. The wood heater pipe was too close to the wall and caught fire. If it hadn't been for the quick response by the Pipestone Fire Department, the whole school might have burned to the ground. The damage was so extensive the school had to be closed down for fear it might collapse.

The school board was faced with quite a dilemma. Now that the school was closed, where were they going to house their students? They held a special school board meeting to discuss the matter. After much discussion, they decided to use city buildings as makeshift classrooms so that the students wouldn't fall behind in their studies. As a result, the students were scattered all over Pipestone, since they had to use several city buildings to accommodate all of them.

CHAPTER 8

Pipestone was now a modern town with many modern conveniences. The problems of the Depression were gradually subsiding. Most of the basic necessities that people had taken for granted were again showing up on store shelves. In fifty years, Pipestone had blossomed. Its elaborate buildings would forever remain its landmark.

The Calumet Hotel, in its early years, was the most swinging place in town. Rumor had it that "Ladies of the Evening" were being brought in from out of town to entertain some of the traveling salesmen in the basement club of the hotel. The salesmen were an integral part of this community's future. They had more clout than the Mayor or any of the City Council members.

Many of the women came from various regions of the country. They were educated, and many of them were extremely beautiful, with exquisite figures. They practiced the world's oldest profession and were good at it. Some of them could match the men drink for drink. Oh, the stories of debauchery the walls of the Calumet Hotel could tell if they could only talk!

The Calumet Hotel became the regular hangout for the men of Pipestone, from the highest officials to the lowliest miners. The hookers were highly experienced and knew not only how to satisfy a man sexually, but also how to bolster his ego. It is no wonder that the Calumet became so popular with the male population of Pipestone.

The rooms of the Calumet were elegantly furnished. Most of the furnishings had been imported by freight from the East, mainly the New England states. The social and economic impact the Calumet Hotel had on this community was incredible.

On Sundays after church, families would gather for brunch in the dining room of the Calumet as musicians softly serenaded them while they dined. Almost everyone was dressed in formal attire. For the children, the Calumet was like a huge castle. While the parents sipped coffee or tea and exchanged philosophical ideas, the children explored the corridors of the hotel. In the meantime, the cleaning ladies frantically cleaned the rooms.

In the dining room, busboys and waitresses were busy clearing the tables in order to accommodate waiting customers. The hotel was always very busy. The service was excellent and the employees were very personable.

Olive Street was a spectacular sight at night with its glowing neon lights. The trucks and cars parked along the streets by the sidewalks made Pipestone look alive and thriving. The streetlights glowed on both sides of the street, illuminating the darkest night. Because of its sidewalks and paved roads, things were looking up around Pipestone. People strolled along the sidewalks hand-in-hand, browsing in local shops. Window-shopping was also an enjoyable pastime on a beautiful autumn night. The children could be heard playing tag and laughing. These were moments to be relished and remembered, because winter was not a welcome season to many of the people of Pipestone. Winters in Pipestone were harsh.

Polly's farmhouse was huge, with eight large rooms and only one wood stove for central heating. Covered by tons of blankets, Polly and her brother Sonny had to sleep together. They both disliked the idea, but had no choice in the matter because it was either bundle up together or freeze to death. So they tried to make the best of it.

Polly and her father would go out to Ihlen Lake and ice fish. Art had built his own ice house. If the day was nice, Polly would put on her ice skates and skate till she got tired. Sometimes she would invite some of her friends, and they would pull a bobsled around the entire lake. She and her friends would build snowmen and have snowball fights. Nice days were rare because most of the time Minnesota's howling winds and frigid temperatures would force Pipestone's inhabitants to stay indoors.

When Polly went fishing with her father, if the fish weren't biting, they would play cards. Polly didn't know how to play cards very well but she tried nonetheless. She was almost ten years old now, and she cherished these special moments with her father.

The year was 1939 and the world was in turmoil. Hitler had just invaded Poland. Two days later, Britain and France declared war on Germany. Two weeks after that, Poland surrendered unconditionally to the Germans. The German war machine was unbelievable. It was lightning fast and attacked with a vengeance. Hitler's mechanized army rolled over the earth, leaving a cloud of dust in its wake and destroying the Polish inhabitants, raping and pillaging like savage animals.

As the rest of the world was recovering from the Depression, Hitler was trying to rule the world, even if it meant destroying innocent lives to satisfy his inflated ego. He was ruthless and cunning. This man possessed the power of the devil. He was out to annihilate the Jews. The Jews were articulate and intelligent, and they were experienced businessmen. The German economy was in financial disarray, but so was the rest of the world.

As the world waited to recover from the Depression, Hitler was building his war machine. The Aryan German brotherhood was assembling and readying itself for the most atrocious carnage that ever befell man. White supremacists felt that they belonged to the perfect race. Their ultimate goal was to eradicate anyone who got in their way. They thought of themselves as invincible. Their audacity was astonishing. Millions of innocent people were destined to die senselessly because of Hitler's demented beliefs. Hitler was an abhorrent tyrant who came from the filthiest part of Vienna, and was considered by most to be a gutter pig and scumbag. He was a despicably evil little man, a wannabe, and a peddler of deceit. He spread his propaganda with its filthy lies, and spent days and nights passing out fliers condemning the Jews for all the world's woes. The Jews had their shit together, but the rest of the world brooded over its shortcomings, particularly the Germans. The poor Jews were exterminated because of these ruthless and misconstrued ideologies disseminated by a man who became the Chancellor of the Third Reich, a man who, by all rights, should have been committed to an asylum for his insanity.

Hitler was a master of deceit who found gullible people to follow his lead. He brainwashed these people into believing he was their savior. Hitler and his followers set out to destroy the world, showing no mercy and no contrition for the atrocities they committed.

America was desperately trying to stay out of the conflict that was beginning to consume the European countries by remaining neutral. But on December 7, 1941, at 7:55 a.m. Hawaiian time, Japan invaded Pearl Harbor, creating havoc and decimating U.S. military forces. The Japanese destroyed most of the naval fleet stationed in Hawaii. This attack signaled the beginning of World War II for the U.S. Tokyo declared war on the United States and Britain. On December 8th, Congress adopted a declaration of war against Japan that propelled the United States into a war they had tried to avoid. On December 11th, Germany and Italy declared war on the United States. The United States was given no choice but to go after Japan with its wide array of weapons. Every able-bodied American male was compelled to fight in defense of his country. The United States would now join Europe and several other countries in defending their freedom from the cowardly nations who struck without warning.

Retaliation came in the form of massive destruction. Japan had sadly underestimated the military prowess of the United States and the loyalty of its people. Unfortunately, many Americans lost their lives defending the country they loved. The men who enlisted in the military came from small towns as well as big cities. Pipestone, Minnesota was one of the towns that sent young soldiers off to war on foreign soil, not knowing if they would return alive or even if they would return at all.

The volatile situation around the globe was such that recruitment of young American males was at an all time high. These young recruits were very naïve and had no inkling of the danger that awaited them. All they knew was that it was their patriotic duty to serve and defend their country and their loved ones. The cries of despondent mothers could be heard around the world as they said good-bye to their sons, and in some cases their daughters, as they went off to war. Some of these mothers would never see their children again. World War II raged on for six long years after Hitler's invasion of Poland.

On April 30, 1945, Adolf Hitler committed suicide in the bunker underneath the Reich Chancellery in Berlin because he was too much of a coward to face the consequences of his abominable crimes against humanity. On May 7, 1945, Germany surrendered unconditionally to the Allies and Russia in a ceremony at Rheims, France. The Japanese Foreign Minister, Mamoru Shigemitsu, and military leaders signed surrender terms on the U.S.S. Missouri in Tokyo Bay. On September 2, 1945, the Germans and Japanese were both soundly defeated by the Allied Forces and the United States. America's possession of the atom bomb became the deterrent against any future world wars.

When all of the victorious American servicemen and women who had served in the Army, Navy, Air Force, and Marines disembarked from the ships docked at New York Harbor, they were welcomed by large crowds of people which included family, friends, and patriotic Americans who where relieved and grateful to have them home. There was a jubilant celebration on the streets of New York. The war was finally over, and in this colossal city there was hugging and kissing even among total strangers. The celebration lasted for days. What these servicemen and women had endured for four grueling years was unfathomable. Only those who had been in the midst of the war could possibly understand what these men and women felt. As these brave men and women returned to their hometown, they were welcomed with parades, bands, laughter, and tears.

Many of our American servicemen and women would never be the same because of what they had experienced during the war. They had changed. Their sufferings had been not only physical, but psychological as well. The physical wounds would in all probability heal, but only God knew if their psychological wounds would ever heal. Now that they were home, they had the job of putting their lives back together again.

CHAPTER 9

During the time that World War II raged on, Polly was busy chasing boys, and developing numerous crushes on a variety of them. She didn't have much luck attaining the boy she really wanted, so Polly and the girls she had befriended formed a girls' club. They called themselves the Thirteen Nifty Teens. There was a very special bond between them. They became inseparable.

Polly's schoolwork continued to suffer because of her obsession with boys. She was constantly daydreaming about romance. She had no doubt that one of the boys she pursued would eventually respond to her. It was just like when her daddy went fishing at the lake. He would sit in his icehouse in temperatures of thirty degrees below zero and wait patiently for the fish to bite, and without fail, they would eventually take the bait.

Polly was in her early teens, and was constantly asking her parents if she could have a dance party at the house. These parties, of course, included boys. To her delight, her parents always said yes. She and her friends, most of whom she had known since kindergarten, would pull out the phonograph and records and move the furniture and rugs out of the living room. They loved to dance to the music of Glenn Miller and his band. Polly and her friends could really swing to that music. Lillian would serve punch and cookies. Hanky panky was not allowed at these parties but once in a while, a daring boy would steal a kiss or two. Alcohol was absolutely forbidden. Lillian was a prim and proper lady who would not tolerate any form of disrespect from Polly's guests.

Lillian didn't quite trust Polly. She would accuse her of drinking and smoking. Polly denied the accusations, and even though she was telling the truth, she got in trouble anyway and would be grounded for a few days.

During one of her parties, Polly got into trouble with her brother Sonny. Evidently Sonny's Glenn Miller album had inadvertently been left on the seat of the sofa, and someone sat on it. Polly had to go all the way to Sioux City, Iowa to buy Sonny a new album before he killed her.

During the war, Sonny had joined the Merchant Marines so he could travel and see the world. Unfortunately, it was hardly the best time to travel and sightsee as the world was in chaos. Merchant Marines were badly needed to deliver supplies around the globe to various military attachments. It was a very dangerous job, but someone had to do it.

Sonny was Lillian's favorite child. In her eyes, he could do no wrong. This favoritism wounded Polly very deeply but she refused to let it show. She didn't like to dwell on it because at those times when she did think about it, especially when her mother was angry with her, she would become very depressed.

Her father, on the other hand, never criticized her, which is why she loved him so much. Polly and her father had a special bond that would last a lifetime.

The high school was sponsoring a dance called Atomize Those Tigers. The school gymnasium was decorated with symbols of the war. Amongst the decorations were replicas of the atomic bombs that had been dropped on Japan on August 6, 1945. The atomic bomb that had been dropped on Hiroshima killing 70,000 people was fourteen feet long, five feet in diameter, and weighed 10,000 pounds. The Enola Gay was the B-29 aircraft that had dropped the atomic bomb. The second bomb was dropped on Nagasaki on August 9, 1945, killing more than 70,000 people. The Nuclear Age had been born, but most of the young kids from Pipestone were oblivious of the happenings during the war. The only thing they knew about the war was the propaganda they heard on the radio. Most of the children who lived in Pipestone led very sheltered lives. Their only interests seemed to be dancing, drinking, driving around in their parents' cars, and making out. Since they took no interest in the war, their world was worry-free.

After the school dance, everyone decided to head towards the quarries near the Three Maidens and neck. For years, the town locals had been using the Three Maidens for their romantic rendezvous. It was the same spot where Nikita had proposed to Winonha before the white man arrived in Minnesota. Polly was among the kids who headed for the Three Maidens. She and a guy named Ken, whom she had had a crush on for a very long time, were making out behind a rock. Ken and Polly had been good friends for a long time, but their relationship was advancing to more than just friendship. They had serious feelings for each other.

Polly wished she lived in town because all the best parties were always held in town. When she was younger, she went to the country school. Her parents wanted her to continue attending the country school but Polly adamantly refused. She said that if she had to, she would walk to school everyday, and she meant it. There was no way in bloody hell she was going to return to the country school when all her friends would be attending the new high school. She walked to school every day. Neither freezing temperatures nor rain nor sleet deterred Polly from walking down that lonely road that lead to the new high school.

Those long silent walks every morning made her think about all the different places she would like to visit. Minneapolis was one of those places she wanted to see. Going to college in the big city intrigued her, but she knew that she had to graduate from high school first. She was having second thoughts about her total commitment to her studies. The thought of having to study Shakespeare was downright depressing. Reading about Romeo and Juliet was boring. She found the language in Shakespeare very confusing, and it seemed to her that the characters were always speaking in riddles. It didn't even sound like English. Polly was not poetically inclined.

On V.J. day, Polly and a few friends decided to ditch school. She had borrowed her brother's car so they could drive to Flandreau, South Dakota. As they drove, they felt like really hot stuff. They spent the whole day in Flandreau running around town as if they owned it. After spending a marvelous day touring the town, they decided it was time to head home. To Polly's dismay, her brother's car had broken down. Evidently she had driven the car without any water in the radiator and had burned the engine. She was in big trouble with her brother, and to top things off, when she returned to school the following day, she got detention.

At home, Polly's parents were livid. They shouted at her, "What the hell were you thinking? Ditching school is bad enough, but ruining your brother's car was inexcusably irresponsible." Lillian's outburst reverberated throughout the house. Her Swedish temper exploded. Polly knew she was in deep trouble. She got grounded for a few days. She really felt bad about what she had done, but she couldn't reverse the situation. Polly would have to suffer the consequences of her actions.

It's a good thing Polly had two aunts who were very fond of her. They had the tendency to spoil her. They bought her new clothes, including a lambskin jacket. She loved the jacket so much that she wore it to school everyday. She was a stylish dresser and never failed to wear her big bows in her hair.

When she was no longer grounded, Ken picked Polly up and they drove around, stopping at the local drug store to buy cherry cokes. They drove to the Three Maidens, which at that time was equivalent to lover's lane, to do some necking. Although things got pretty hot and heavy, the thought of pregnancy deterred them from engaging in intercourse. They were quite aware that a few moments of sexual pleasure could lead to a lifetime of parenthood.

Whenever Ken took Polly home, he would park in front of the house and they would sit in the car necking. Polly's father would flash the lights on and off as a signal that it was time for Polly to get into the house. Sometimes the signal went unheeded because Polly and Ken were much too busy to notice. Ever since Polly could remember, she had been curious about kissing. Ken satisfied her curiosity and she was not in the least bit disappointed.

When her father approached the car, the windows were all fogged up. He softly rapped on the window and said in a low tone, "It's time to come into the house, Polly." She passionately kissed Ken one last time before getting out of the car. Her whole body was on fire. She wanted to experience the ecstasy of lovemaking, but at least for now, she would have to wait.

When Polly went to bed that night, all she could think about was Ken. She cuddled with her pillow, pretending it was Ken. She lay there fantasizing about Ken and what sexual intercourse with him would feel like. She finally fell asleep and dreamed that he was making love to her. He was masterfully arousing every one of her erogenous zones. His kisses were feverishly passionate. Her dream was so erotic that she actually experienced several orgasms as she slept. When she awoke, her heart was fiercely beating and her pillow was completely soaked. Her dream had been so realistic that she was, for the moment, sexually satisfied. The following day at school, Polly looked at Ken in a whole different light. Because of her dream, she wanted Ken even more than before.

She was still committed to the Thirteen Nifty Teens (TNT). Doris was Polly's best friend, and then there was Janis, Joyce, Beverly, Emily Ann, Maryanne, Valerie, Lucille, Jerry, and the three Donna's. Everyone in school was envious of their clique. There were quite a few girls who wanted to join this elite club, but thirteen was a lucky number and they didn't dare break it.

Polly was a lot taller than Ken. Some of the other boys felt self-conscious being around her because she was much taller, but Ken didn't seem to mind being shorter than Polly.

The parties in town were always a lot more fun. Everything was more modern and many of the houses had beautiful lawns, flowers, and trees, and were beautifully landscaped. All the streets, sidewalks, and paved roads were lit up. The bright lights made everything more inviting. Polly and Doris attended some of the parties in town but Polly had a curfew. Her parents were very protective. If she lost track of time and didn't make it home by curfew, her father would crash the party and remind Polly that it was time to get home, which she did.

Polly wanted desperately to live in town. One Friday night, Polly decided to have another country dance while her parents went bowling. Almost every kid in town attended Polly's country party. Some of the kids who were on their way to the party decided to play a prank on Polly, so they collected all the beer and whiskey bottles that were strewn along the ditch and put them behind the curtain on the window sill. They thought it was funny, but when the party was over, Lillian found the liquor bottles. Polly was in deep trouble once again. She tried to tell her mother that there had been no liquor at her party, but Lillian refused to believe her. As far as Lillian was concerned, Polly was headed down a very destructive path. Polly tried pleading with her mother, saying, "Mother, there was no drinking going on at last night's party. Honest!" But, Lillian having caught her in so many lies already, didn't believe her. Polly said, "Fine, don't believe me!" and stormed out the door madder than hell and headed towards her grandmother's.

She related the incident to her grandmother, saying by way of explanation, "As a prank, some of the guys who attended the party last night planted empty bottles of liquor where they were sure my mother would find them. My mother doesn't believe me and will probably never let me have another country dance at the house." Polly's eyes were red from crying as the tears continued to roll down her cheeks. In her Swedish accent, Polly's grandmother said, "Don't worry, darling, I'll have a talk with your mother and try to straighten out this misunderstanding." Polly hugged her grandmother, who was now a foot shorter than Polly. Unfortunately, Lillian wouldn't budge. She wasn't buying any of it and had lost her trust in Polly.

On Monday, everyone who had attended the party met at the school canteen to discuss the weekend's fiasco. Polly wanted to know who the scoundrels were who had had the audacity to play such a cruel prank. Her eyes scanned the faces of the guys who were there, hoping to see some sign of guilt in the culprits. To her dismay, she came up empty.

The canteen was a good place for the school kids to hang out and socialize with their friends. There was a pool table and a jukebox. Some of the kids danced to the music playing on the jukebox, some of them played pool, and others just talked. Polly, in the meantime, was still seething at having to take heat from her mother for something she didn't do. She was determined to find out who had played the nasty prank.

When Polly got home, Lillian had calmed down, and gave her a hug to let her know that all was forgiven. She had loving parents who couldn't stay mad at her for very long. All things considered, she was lucky to have such loving and understanding parents and a dog who adored her. Sally was always there when Polly was feeling down and needed a friend. Her dog was quite sensitive to her moods. She would sit on Polly's lap when she sensed Polly was depressed, and Polly would whisper in Sally's ear how much she loved her and how much she valued their special bond.

In the meantime, Lillian would be in the kitchen fixing supper. Art was a hard-working farmer who worked his fingers to the bone in order to provide for his family. Hard work was all he knew. Art believed that hard work never hurt anybody, and his life was proof of this belief. Even though they were poor, Art and Lillian were highly respected by citizens of Pipestone.

CHAPTER 10

Pipestone was going through a modernization period. Dress fashions were becoming more radical among the youth, and Polly was there to lead the way. She was a natural trendsetter. It was her destiny to lead, not to follow. Polly had inexhaustible energy and infectious enthusiasm. She had an insatiable need to be the center of attention. The boys were more than willing to provide this attention, but at that time the attention she most wanted was from Ken.

Ken worked at the local hardware store after school and on weekends. He earned $13.00 a week and worked rigorous hours. He knew that twenty-three cents an hour was just not enough, and he needed to figure out a way to supplement his income.

He eventually saved enough money to buy a 1933 Plymouth Coupe with a rumble seat. When he first bought it, he and his best friend, J. Wesley Ellingson, cruised around to show off his new car. He was quite proud of it. It was a beautiful Sunday afternoon, and after church services, the people were strolling along the sidewalks of Pipestone. Olive Street was filled with joyous laughter and lively conversation. As Ken cruised the street, he revved the engine of his car, wanting to attract the attention of his friends. They waved at him as he drove by.

As he drove down one of the streets, he saw a group of his friends standing near a fire hydrant, so he pulled over. Needless to say, they were quite impressed with Ken's new car and started asking all kinds of questions such as where did he buy it, what kind of engine did it have, and so forth. He answered as best he could, but thoughts of Polly kept distracting him. He was crazy about her, and no matter how hard he tried to focus on the conversation at hand, it became quite impossible. He decided to go to her house so she could see his new acquisition.

When Ken arrived at Polly's house, he honked a couple of times, hoping she would be the one to come out. After awhile Polly appeared. With a smile that lit up her face, she asked Ken if the car was his. When he told her it was, she asked when he was going to take her for a ride in it. He said, "Right now if you'd like." She told him she had to get permission from her parents but that she would be right back. She dashed into the house and returned a few minutes later, got into the car where she sat beside Ken, and they were off. Polly told Ken that she really liked his new car. He turned the radio on, and Polly cuddled closer to Ken as they drove towards Pipestone. They drove all around Pipestone showing off Ken's new car.

As they drove around, Polly asked Ken what he thought about getting everybody together and driving down to Hatfield, where they could go dancing at the Hollyhock Ballroom. The following day at school, word went around that everybody was going dancing in Hatfield. The hallways were buzzing with excitement and the girls were planning what to wear.

Emily Anne asked Polly, "Do you think I should wear my saddle shoes?" Polly replied, "Yes. I think they would look great with that new outfit you bought the other day." Since all the girls considered Polly a fashion authority, they kept asking her opinion on what they should wear to the dance. Polly's usual response was, "Wear whatever you feel comfortable in."

On Friday, everyone gathered in front of Mr. Bennett's drug store dressed in what they considered their most fashionable clothes. The girls wore their best dresses and saddle shoes; the boys wore their nicest slacks, white shirts, and be-bop shoes. There were fourteen couples and four cars to accommodate them. There was a great deal of excitement as the kids piled into the cars anticipating a fun-filled evening.

These teenagers had grown up within the confines of Pipestone and had no idea what other towns were like. Tonight they would find out. The radios in the cars blared as they headed towards Hatfield. Polly intermittently kissed Ken's cheek as he drove, causing him to lose concentration on his driving. J. Ellington and Emily Anne were in the back seat of Ken's car kissing while the other couples teased them about coming up for air. They were too busy with each other to pay attention to anyone else. "Fun" was the only thing on the kids' minds as they drove into Hatfield, whose population was 150 people. They drove directly to the Hollyse Hawk Ballroom.

When all four cars arrived, everyone entered the large ballroom with wooden floors. The lights were dimmed and a few couples were already slow dancing to Lawrence Welk. Suddenly, the sounds of Glenn Miller brought the place to life. Ken and Polly were the first ones on the dance floor. These two could really jitterbug. The "Lindy" was another dance the kids like to dance to. Everyone was dancing, sweating, and having a great time. All too soon, the evening was over. Already the kids were planning their next escapade to Hatfield. Dancing was a great passion for the kids from Pipestone. Every chance they got, they planned a dance at someone's house on the weekend.

The older generation considered the jitterbug a vulgar display and greatly disapproved of this new craze. For the kids, it was a great way to expend their pent-up energy. They were good kids and saw nothing wrong with the jitterbug.

Polly and her friends continued their involvement in the Thirteen Nifty Teens Club. Most of the members belonged to prominent families. Emily Anne was the thirteenth and last member to be inducted into the sorority that inspired the name of the club. She and her family had just moved to Pipestone from South Dakota. Polly and Emily Anne developed an instant friendship, and Polly made sure Emily Anne was accepted into the Club. Polly was quite popular in Pipestone, so for Emily Anne, having Polly as a friend was quite an advantage.

Emily Anne came from a large family. She dearly loved her brothers and sisters, but with so many of them, there just wasn't enough of the individual attention that she craved. She had an uncle who lived in Pipestone. His name was James Manion and he was the County Attorney. He had a wife and two children. His wife took care of all of the domestic chores. Being a good seamstress, she sewed most of the clothes for her children. Unfortunately her health wasn't good, so Mr. Manion had to find someone to help her with some of the housework. As Emily Anne had always been their favorite niece, they asked Emily Anne's parents if Emily could live with them for a while. James Manion said he would support her, and he and his wife would care for her like a daughter. Emily Anne was ecstatic and packed post haste. This was her chance to get the space and privacy that she desperately wanted but couldn't get at home.

The first few days after she moved in with her aunt and uncle were a bit unsettling because she wasn't used to the quiet, but she knew it was what she needed at this time in her life. Emily came from a very poor family and her wardrobe was quite sparse. All she had were a few dresses which had been handed down to her from her sisters. Now that she was living with her Uncle Manion, she felt very self-conscious wearing her hand-me-downs. She instinctively knew that from now on things would be different. Her aunt and uncle were quite generous with her. They not only bought her new clothes, they also gave her the love and attention she craved.

On her first day at Jasper-Pipestone High School, she felt very awkward and alone. The first person to befriend her was none other than Polly. She and Polly hit it off right away. Emily Anne was witty, very intelligent, quite attractive, and had a winning personality. With very little trouble, she became one of the most popular girls in school and a model student. She also caught the eye of one of the most popular guys in school, J. Ellington. It was a case of mutual attraction. She was elated at the way the kids from Jasper and Pipestone had so warmly accepted her. Her life was changing for the better.

As much as she loved her family, her reclusive life at home with her parents and so many brothers and sisters had been a nightmare. She wanted more. All the attention she was now getting was overwhelming, and she loved it. She and Polly had developed a special friendship that would span a lifetime.

It was a weekend, and Ken, Polly, J. Ellington, Emily Anne, and a few other friends were partying and just driving around. They had just left the quarry near the Three Maidens where they had been necking for most of the night. They decided to take a long drive out in the country. Ken's car was packed with four couples. As they drove along a country road in the middle of nowhere, Ken suddenly stopped, got out of the car, and suggested that everyone get out and dance in the middle of the road. The others thought he had lost his mind as he turned up the volume of the car radio. The moon was quite bright and the stars twinkled to the beat of the music.

Ken and Polly began to dance, and the others followed their lead. They were jitterbugging and hopping around like a bunch of lunatics. In reality, they weren't bad kids. Having grown up in a small town with very little action, they were just creating their own fun in an effort to stave off boredom.

With the Prom not too far away, the school was buzzing on the subject. The guys began securing their dates. Polly was walking down the hall with a few friends when a guy named Jim Jordan walked up to her and asked if she would like to be his date for the Prom. Without a second thought, she said, "Yes." Jim had a terrific personality and was a great dancer. Ken would just have to ask someone else.

The night of the Prom, Jim picked Polly up at her house. He was wearing a black tuxedo and looked quite handsome. Polly looked stunning in the red and white formal that she wore. When Jim and Polly walked into the high school gymnasium, they looked great. There was, however, something wrong with the picture. Polly was Ken's girl and everybody knew it. As the saying goes, though, "You snooze, you lose." Jim had beaten Ken to the punch. Polly still loved Ken, but she wasn't about to wait around till he decided to ask her to the Prom. Besides, Polly wasn't ready to commit to just one guy. She was much to young for such a serious commitment.

The music blared from the loudspeakers as the kids in all their regalia waited for someone to make the first move and begin dancing. As the couples stood looking around at each other, Polly knew she would have to be the one to get the Prom going, so she pulled Jim by the hand to the middle of the dance floor. She and Jim danced great together.

Ken had invited a girl named Millie to the Prom. He tried to pretend he didn't care that Polly was there with someone else, but when he thought she wasn't looking, he couldn't help but glance at her. He sure missed being with her. Millie was fun, but she wasn't Polly. Ken had taken his relationship with Polly for granted, and at this moment he greatly regretted it. Polly would not be taken for granted, and Ken had learned this lesson the hard way. This was a mistake he was not about to make again. It pained him to see Polly in another man's arms. He was totally jealous. He couldn't stand seeing her have so much fun with someone else. Until this moment, he hadn't realized how much he loved Polly.

Polly was having a great time. Jim was a marvelous dancer and loads of fun to be with. The evening was turning out to be everything she hoped it would be. She was having so much fun with Jim, she hadn't even thought about Ken. The Prom ended all too quickly. Jim took Polly home, and before she went into the house, kissed her gently on the lips. Polly was never allowed to stay out past midnight so, at the stroke of twelve, her magically wonderful evening ended.

The following day was Saturday. Ken called Polly to ask if she would like to go for a ride with him. She said she'd love to. When Ken picked her up at her house, he told her how much he loved her and how much he had missed being with her the previous night. Polly was flattered and cuddled next to him as they drove off. They cruised around for a while, and then stopped at the drugstore. Everyone in the drugstore was talking about how exciting the Prom had been. Some of them bragged about how they had frolicked till dawn near the Maidens, and how most of them had stayed out all night. This made Ken and Polly a little jealous. They vowed that they would stay out all night for the Prom next year regardless of what their parent said. Ken and Polly ordered cheeseburgers and cherry colas, and as they ate, their friends continued bragging about the previous night's events.

Winter would soon be upon them. In this region, winters always proved to be harsh and frigid to the point where cars were difficult to start. The winters in this part of the country were so cold that the car heaters didn't work very well. Ken cursed to himself as he cruised around because it was colder in the car than it was outside. He rolled down the windows in an effort to keep the windshield from fogging up. It was starting to snow, and as the large flakes landed on the windshield, the wipers were having a heck of a time clearing them off.

The way the snow swirled around was a good indication that the oncoming snowstorm was going to leave a lot of snow on the ground. "Think Snow" was most definitely not one of Pipestone's mottos because there were no mountains for skiing or sledding. In fact, the tremendous amount of snow that Pipestone got only served to cause hardship and misery to both man and beast.

Ken knew that the snowflakes that were now falling heralded a vicious storm. At least six inches of snow had already fallen, and there was no indication the storm would be letting up any time soon. Polly lived a few miles south of town, and Ken knew that if he waited much longer to take her home they would be snowbound. It was snowing quite heavily, and the winds were making the car rock violently back and forth. After dropping Polly off at her house, he barely made it home himself.

It snowed two days in a row, and the wind gusts created eight-foot snowdrifts in some places. Many people were left stranded. Pipestone was in a state of emergency. Farmers were vigorously working to shelter their animals in an effort to keep them from freezing to death. This horrendous two-day snowstorm blanketed the earth. Many people were trapped inside their homes. The snow was so deep that it had sealed the doorways. Pipestone was completely paralyzed. Ken and his father shoveled snow for three days just so they could get out of the driveway.

What attracted people to this desolate region is incomprehensible. The white man was now experiencing what the Indian had known for thousands of years.

As always, after the miseries of winter dissipated, the people of the northern plains enjoyed the beauty of springtime. After a long winter and bouts of cabin fever, some of the kids would get a little wild. They'd spent most of the winter cooped up, so who could blame them?

Emily Anne and J. Ellington started dating seriously. His car was kind of beat up and the roof had a gaping hole, but he and Emily didn't care as they rode around town. While they were cruising, dark gray clouds sped across the fading blue sky. Within minutes an eerie gray atmosphere enveloped them. With very little warning, they were caught in a torrential downpour that took them by surprise. The hole in the roof of the car, which hadn't bothered them minutes before, was cause for concern now. The rain poured into the car through the hole, soaking not only the car, but its two passengers as well. Being young and in love has its merits. Emily Anne had her umbrella, which she opened to protect them from the continuing rain as she and J. Ellington continued cruising around town. They laughed till they cried as the rain kept pouring in through the hole in the roof.

The heavy spring rains were far more welcome than the unmercifully cold winters. The sloshing sound of tires treading water created a soothing rhythm. Small rivers formed along the roadside where larger rivers were created as the water accumulated. By the time Emily Anne got home, every inch of her body was wet. For Emily Anne and J. Ellington this would be one of those memorable times that would forever be etched in their hearts.

Emily Anne was hopelessly in love with J. Ellington, and would lie in bed at night fantasizing about what her life would be like with him. She also dreamed about all the children they would have someday.

Unfortunately, even though they were seriously dating, Emily Anne knew that in all probability they would never be lovers because the family she lived with was very strict. They kept her busy cooking, cleaning, doing laundry, and making sure the children were fed. Mrs. Manion had become ill, and since she was unable to care for herself or her family any longer, she had been placed in a hospital. Emily Anne was now in charge of all the household duties. After school, she had to clean the house, tend to the children, cook, and wash the dishes. At the end of her long arduous day, she still had to do her homework. When she was done, the hour was late and she was totally exhausted.

The school year began to wind down. There was one week left before Polly and her classmates completed their junior year. They were looking forward to summer vacation. Polly was not exactly an avid student, so she was especially glad when the school year ended. She was amazed and thrilled that she passed her courses and would be a senior the following year. Given her aversion to studying, she considered herself fortunate to have made it this far.

The years had flown by so quickly. In her more pensive moods, Polly recalled with fondness all the friends she had made along the way and the fun times they had shared. Even though she didn't care all that much for school, she treasured the friends she had made. The thought of being separated from them made her feel somewhat uneasy. She would especially miss the Thirteen Nifty Teens because she and the other twelve members had been together since kindergarten and had formed a special bond. She would miss them dearly. They had learned to tolerate each other's quirks and differences in personality. It had started out as a little girls' club formed just for fun but had evolved into a circle of everlasting friendship.

Polly was bored. She told her mother it was time she found a job so she could start earning her own money. She had begun to feel a deep-seated need for independence. She had one more year of high school to complete, and was already fantasizing about moving into her own apartment in Minneapolis. She adored her parents but felt they were at times a little too strict. She was ready to spread her wings and fly on her own.

CHAPTER 11

Polly got a job at Northwestern Bell as a part-time telephone operator. She loved her new job, where she worked late into the afternoon, and on occasion, late into the evening. Ken and a few other friends would sneak in the back door to see Polly while she worked. She loved the attention she received from her friends. These were the best years in Polly's life.

On her days off, she and her friends would get together and go out to Big Benton Lake where they swam and water-skied. Some of the guys would go fishing. The Minnesota summers were great. There were lakes everywhere and more native fish than you could shake a stick at. The high rising heat wave that came off the water made everything seem so serene. It sure beat the hell out of those bitter cold winter days. When the sun had set, they would build a large bonfire and the guys would cook the fish they had caught. They also cooked hot dogs and hamburgers. The radio would be on and they would dance around the bonfire to the music that was playing. A fiery red silhouette reflected off the water as the moon shone high in the heavens, and the glow of the stars made the evening seductively romantic. The couples were kissing, embracing, and wishing time would stand still.

On another weekend, Ken, Polly and a few of their friends decided to drive to Sioux Falls, South Dakota to a dance at the Arkota Ballroom. The Lindy, a new dance, was all the rage. The band that would be performing was the Jimmy Dorsey Band. Big band had become quite popular with the younger generation. Kids arrived in droves from all the surrounding communities. Dancing was a great form of exercise as well as a constructive and fun way of expending pent-up energy.

Everyone was awed by the magnificent splendor of the Arkota Ballroom. It attracted some of the biggest names in the entertainment business such as Louis Armstrong, Tommy Dorsey, and Jimmy Dorsey. The ballroom was always packed. Everyone was dressed in formal attire and looked very attractive.

Most of the band members were already on stage tuning their instruments. No sooner did the music begin when couples rushed to fill the dance floor. An intense energy filled the ballroom and the floor began to shake under dancing feet. Ken and Polly were in their own little world. Whether it was infatuation or true love, they savored the delicious feeling. After the dance, they all went to eat at an all-night restaurant, after which they drove back to Pipestone.

Polly worked the entire summer. When Lillian, Polly's mother, was younger, she was the supervisor of the telephone operators at Northwestern Bell. Once she and Art were married, she decided to stay home and raise a family.

Summer came to an end, and Polly returned to school to complete her senior year. Not being academically inclined, she concentrated more on her social life than on her studies. She loathed schoolwork and wanted to take the least demanding courses, so she chose vocational training. She attended school in the mornings and worked at Northwestern Bell in the afternoons.

Sadly, the Thirteen Nifty Teens Club was on its last legs. This would be the last year the club would be in existence, so the members huddled in the hallway in an effort to be together as much as they could. While the student body was busy planning all the students' activities for the school year, the TNT girls were busy planning the parties and dances for the year.

Ken and Polly continued dating steadily during their senior year. Ken was forever showing up at Polly's house in a different car each time. He made better money buying and selling cars than working at the hardware store. Ken was madly in love with Polly, and was convinced that he would end up marrying her someday. Polly seemed to share the same feelings, at least for the moment. There was definitely a strong sexual attraction between them. One of the times they were at their favorite spot, they began kissing, embracing, and caressing. He lay on top of her and pressed his body against hers. She responded with equal urgency. They were in a frenzy of wild passion. They both climaxed, and as they lay trembling in each other's arms, neither one could believe the incredibly sensual feelings they had just experienced. They were both sweating profusely as they held tightly to each other. Their faces were aglow as they smiled at one another and professed their love. Later that night as they lay in their own beds, they could think only of each other, and they knew it had been a night neither one would easily forget.

For years Polly had walked three-and-a-half miles to school through the cold winter months and rainy spring days. Now, however, Ken had become her chauffeur and she loved it. He would pick her up after school and take her cruising up and down Olive Street. Before driving her to work, he would take her to the local drugstore for a refreshment. When Polly got off work, Ken would be there to drive her home. Sally, her dog, would be waiting for her at the gate. Polly would swoop her up and cradle her in her arms, all the while talking to her in baby talk that Sally seemed to understand. Polly also had two ducks named Chester and Lester, a goat, a lamb, and a goose. She babied all of them as if they were her children.

Polly had a heart of gold and was very popular in school. At some indeterminate point in her senior year, Polly's wild streak disappeared. In the past, Polly had been the type of person who wanted to be in ten places at once, which was virtually impossible, but she tried anyway. Now she was a bit more docile.

This time when the Prom came around, Ken asked Polly immediately because he didn't want to make the same mistake he had made the last time. Polly accepted without hesitation. On Prom night, Ken picked Polly up at seven o'clock sharp. As he pulled up to her house, he felt his heart skip a beat. He was a little nervous, which was out of character for him. Polly was his girl, and they had been dating for a couple of years. He felt secure in their relationship and couldn't understand why his stomach was tied up in knots. With corsage in hand he knocked on the door a couple of times before Art, Polly's father, answered. He said, "Good evening, Ken. How are you this evening?" Ken replied, "I'm fine, thank you sir."

It was a lie because he didn't feel fine; he was nervous as hell. Art invited him into the living room and asked him to have a seat. He said Polly would be right down.

Ken was wearing a thin dark blue wool suit that accented his blonde hair and blue eyes. When Polly walked into the room, Ken's face lit up. She looked stunning in a long black lace formal gown that flared out and black patent leather shoes. Her gown was accented by the beautiful pearl necklace and matching earrings she wore. On her head was a black velvet bow. The black gown she wore revealed her soft creamy skin. For a moment, Ken seemed to be freezing this very special moment in time. The sight of her left him speechless. When his speech returned, he told Polly how beautiful she looked. She smiled at him and returned the compliment. Ken gave Polly the corsage and helped her pin it on. They smiled nervously at each other. Art got his camera and took pictures of them before they left.

After all the formalities, they were finally on their way to one of their most important dates, the Senior Prom. It was considered the grand gala of Jasper-Pipestone High School. Ken drove down the infamous Olive Street, where other kids were already cruising. There had been a rumor going around that most of the seniors were planning to stay out all night.

Before long, everyone began to arrive at the Prom. The scent of perfume permeated the air, creating an aura of sensuality, excitement, and anticipation. The girls looked regal in their chic evening gowns, and the guys were quite handsome in their suits and ties.

The first dance was a slow one, and as the music began to play, couples started to dance. The following song was far more upbeat. Ken and Polly started jitterbugging. They looked really good together. Ken twirled Polly on the dance floor as the other kids formed a circle around them. They were the best dancers in school, and looked almost like professionals. Ken and Polly were the life of the party. The onlookers began to clap as their dance steps became more creative. They didn't even get winded! Polly and Ken were having a great time as they danced the night away. They were having so much fun, they didn't want the evening to end. This would be their last Prom and they wanted to make the most of every precious moment.

When the Prom ended, everyone went to the favorite hangout near the Three Maidens. The guys gathered wood and built a fire. It was late October and the nights were uncomfortably chilly. Some of the kids had bottles of booze, which they started to pass around. Most of the kids were drinking, but when the bottle reached Ken and Polly, they didn't take a drink. Everyone was standing around the bonfire in formal attire, drinking, and trying to keep warm. The plan was to keep the bonfire going all night. It didn't take long for the alcohol to start having an effect on the kids who were drinking. Their speech became slurred and incoherent. It was nearing midnight and time for Polly to go home. She and Ken wanted to stay out all night like the rest of their friends, but they knew their parents would not allow it, so they drove home.

As they headed down the road, Polly sat close to Ken. She put her arm around him and gently nibbled at his ear as she whispered, thanking him for a most wonderful evening. He thanked her as well. When he pulled up in front of her house, everything was in complete darkness. Not even the moon was out. The wind blew hard enough to shake the car and rattle the windows. Ken reached for Polly and gave her a long, passionate kiss. They continued kissing till her father turned the porch light on and off. The night was officially over. They exchanged thanks for a most wonderful evening. Polly couldn't remember a more memorable night than this one.

Polly was crazy about Ken, and tried to imagine what her life would be like married to him and having his children. She was still a virgin, and the thought of sexual intimacy excited her. Her sexual desires were getting stronger, but she knew that she would have to keep them under control until she married.

Between school and her part-time job with Northwestern Bell, Polly was in a rut. There wasn't enough excitement in her life and she was becoming desperately bored. She hated school even more now that she was a senior. She was failing chemistry and English literature. Her teachers kept warning her that if her grades didn't improve, she wouldn't be able to graduate with the rest of the Senior Class. Their warnings went in one ear and out the other.

The school counselor telephoned Polly's father and informed him that his daughter was failing most of her classes and would not be graduating with the Senior Class. When Polly got home from work that evening, her father told her that she wasn't going to graduate. She asked her father if he would call her teachers and ask if there was some way she could make up her deficiencies. So Art called Polly's teachers, who told him the only way she would be able to pass the classes she was failing was to score a "C" or better on her exams. Polly became obsessed with the thought that she had to ace the tests. The following Monday, Polly took the exams, and to her relief, passed them all. She couldn't believe how close she had come to not graduating.

On graduation night, Polly and the Thirteen Nifty Teens were ecstatic and yet a bit sad. They were over-joyed at having reached the moment they had anticipated for so long, but they were saddened by the thought that the Thirteen Nifty Teens club would be disbanded.

During the ceremony, the graduates were teary-eyed as they walked up to the podium to receive their diplomas. Cheers could be heard from the audience. When the ceremony ended, there were parties all over Pipestone. While at a party that night, Polly smoked her first cigarette and drank her first beer. It was the first time she had ever gotten drunk. Her mom was convinced that she had been drinking all along, but the truth was that this was the first time for Polly. She was eighteen years old now and was going to move out of her parents' house. For the longest time she had dreamed of being on her own. In her opinion, her parents had been far too strict, and she desperately wanted her independence.

A week after graduation, Polly moved into her own apartment in Pipestone. She had spoken to her parents about her desire to move out, and with their blessing, that's exactly what she did. The apartment she had chosen was small, but it suited her just fine. Her parents and her brother helped her move all her belongings into her new apartment, and even bought her groceries and a few other necessities she would need.

The first night in her apartment, she invited a few friends over to show off her apartment. They were thrilled for her as well as for the fact that now they would have a place to hang out and party. The guys brought the libations while Polly, Emily Anne, Doris and Janis supplied the snacks.

Polly was relieved and overjoyed at finally being out of high school. Having her own apartment made Polly feel very grown up, self-sufficient and invincible. Life was good! The only thing she wasn't sure about was her relationship with Ken. The last time they were together, Ken had proposed marriage. She finally had her freedom and was not ready to make a lifetime commitment. She was having too much fun to be tied down to one man. Ken, on the other hand, was head over heels in love with Polly but felt their relationship was no longer on very solid ground.

Polly's newly found freedom produced a feeling of excitement and elation that coursed through her. She was out to conquer the world, and she refused to let anyone stand in her way. She was her own person and was determined to do things her way, and if she made mistakes along the way, she would deal with them.

Feeling daring, Polly began smoking, drinking, and carousing with men she barely knew. She was an extremely attractive and sexy woman. One Friday evening, Polly gave a party at her apartment. In the course of the evening, she met a man named Josh Goodman. Josh was tall, dark, and extremely handsome, with wavy black hair and a thin slick mustache. He had the physique of a college football player. He had shown up with one of Polly's friends. The minute he walked in, there was total silence as all eyes turned to look at this Adonis. He had captured the attention of every female guest at the party. When he spoke, his deep melodious voice was mesmerizing.

Polly, who was buzzed by now, walked over to him and introduced herself. As they sized each other up, an instant attraction developed. She offered him a beer, which he gratefully accepted. They were captivated by each other to the point where they became totally oblivious of everyone else in the room. Polly had become completely spellbound by this beautiful stranger. They walked into the hallway, where he took her in his arms and gently kissed her lips. She went weak in the knees as his tongue explored her mouth. He pressed his body roughly against her. She could feel the warm moisture running down her leg. Her sexual desire grew under his expert manipulation. He pulled her dress up and pulled down her underwear. He unzipped his pants, pulled out his penis, and gently entered her. The pain was unbearably delightful as she screamed in ecstasy. The deeper he entered, the more she screamed. With one last thrust it was over. She cried as her body fell limply against him.

Polly had just given her virginity to a complete stranger. He kissed her lips one last time and was gone. He left her standing there looking at the blood running down her leg. Her screams had attracted the attention of some of her guests, and as they looked into the hallway, they knew what had happened. She felt so guilty and ashamed she just wanted to disappear.

As she ran into her apartment, she asked everyone to please leave – the party was over. Polly couldn't remember ever feeling so ashamed. Her reputation was a high price to pay for her one moment of indiscretion. By tomorrow the whole town would know that she had had sex with a total stranger. She walked into the bathroom and ran the water so she could take a bath. She felt cheap and dirty. As she bathed, she sobbed uncontrollably at the thought of being condemned by the entire town. The good thing was that it was a weekend and she could stay cloistered in her room. The following day, friends came by to see how she was doing but she wouldn't answer the door. She just wanted to die!

All her life she had saved herself for the man she married. She always dreamed that her husband would be the first man to make love to her on their wedding night. In her state of despair she wondered what decent man would want her now that she was "used goods". How was she going to face her friends? They would probably be discussing what they had seen. The more she thought about it, the more convinced she became that the only way out was to leave Pipestone. She had always wanted to live in Minneapolis.

On Sunday morning, she called her parents to come pick her up so she could go out and visit the farm. What she needed right now was family. During her visit that Sunday, her parents told her that they were going to Texas on vacation, and asked if she wanted to accompany them. She agreed, and asked if she could invite her friend Laura to come along to keep her company. Her parents said they thought it would be a great idea.

On Monday when she went to work, she asked her supervisor if she could take a few days off so she could go on vacation with her parents. Her supervisor approved her leave, and on Wednesday she and her family left for Texas, driving down a desolate road across Iowa.

It was Polly's first trip away from home. This part of the country was so flat you could see for miles and miles. Every farmhouse looked like the one they had just passed. There were many small lakes along the road. Next to a three-story old white Victorian home was a large barn, and in front of the home was a huge lake with clear blue water. The scattered cumulus clouds cast shadows on the water. The rays of sun touching the water made it glisten like diamonds. Next to the lake was a very large grassy meadow with a herd of cows idly grazing.

As Art and Lillian continued to drive across the barren plains of Iowa, Polly knew that this trip was a great idea because the farther away they got from Pipestone, her ordeal seemed less real. She still couldn't believe she had given herself to a complete stranger, and she felt bad that she and Ken had grown apart.

After several days on the road, they arrived at Three Rivers, Texas. This was a business trip for Art, but he had decided to take the family along so they could enjoy a much-needed vacation. It had been a long time since they had gone anywhere. They all needed time away from the farm.

Three Rivers, Texas was such a small town that if you blinked your eyes, you'd miss it. There was one motel, where they rented a room so they could wash off the dust and the sweat as well as get a good night's rest, and then continue on towards their destination. Brownsville was still quite a distance away. This rural town was so small and isolated that gossip seemed to be its favorite form of entertainment. Everyone knew each other's business.

By the time they cleaned up, it was twilight. They walked across the street to the only café in town to get a bite to eat. As they walked into the café, which was small but very clean, a hostess ushered them to a corner booth situated in the back. A couple of young cowboys sitting at one of the tables caught Laura's and Polly's attention. These were authentic cowboys, not wannabes. As they ate, the two cowboys and the two girls kept eyeing each other. When they had finished eating, the handsome cowboys approached the table where Laura and Polly were sitting. They introduced themselves and told the girls that there was going to be a dance that night. They wanted to know if Laura and Polly would like to go.

Later that night, the cowboys, Matt and Billy, picked Laura and Polly up at the motel. They were nineteen-year-olds who drove a Ford pickup truck and spoke with a deep Southern accent. Matt and Billy both had a mouth full of chewing tobacco. The girls thought they were cute but different. When they arrived at the local dance hall, everyone wanted to know who the two raving beauties were. Matt and Billy introduced them to all their friends, who spoke with the same Southern accent.

The dance hall was big, but didn't compare to the ballrooms in Minnesota. In comparison, the ballrooms back home made the dance hall look like a matchbox. A local band was playing country and western music. Billy took Polly by the hand and led her to the middle of the dance floor, where they jitterbugged honky-tonk style. Polly was a natural born dancer and was gracefully flaunting it. She was good enough to be a dance instructor. The girls never imagined they could have this much fun in a small hick town.

The following day, the family left for Brownsville. The terrain across Texas was just as flat as the northern plains states. The drive was hot and humid even with the windows rolled down. It was miserable. They couldn't drink enough water to quench their thirst. It was late in the evening when they arrived in Brownsville. The temperature cooled off a little but they could still feel the sticky sweat on their bodies. The clinging beads of sweat on their bodies made them feel very uncomfortable. They desperately needed a cool shower and a change of clothes.

Brownsville was the largest city they had ever been to. The glow of the neon lights and streetlights made the city look like it was on fire. They drove into the main business district and found a very nice southwestern style motel. In the middle of the courtyard there was a large swimming pool. The area around the pool was landscaped with a variety of cacti and other desert plants. The rooms were clean and fairly large. Everybody cleaned up, had a nice dinner and went to a movie.

The following morning they went sightseeing, after which they drove to a very large ranch just outside the city limits. They rode horses most of the afternoon despite the fact that they had very little riding experience. They were all having a good time. Polly was having so much fun on this vacation she didn't want it to end. She really didn't want to return to Pipestone just yet. Her illicit affair with a complete stranger still haunted her. Small towns had no secrets, and she knew tongues would still be wagging when she got home. But after spending a week in Texas, it was time to return home.

Polly knew she couldn't hide forever, so when she returned to Pipestone, she went back to work at the telephone company. She asked her father to buy her a car so that he wouldn't have to drive her to and from work. Her father agreed to her request with the stipulation that she pay him back. He went shopping for a car, and ended up buying an older model Ford coupe. Polly had to pay him ten dollars a month with the agreement that if she failed to make a payment, he would take the car away from her.

Having her own car gave Polly a sense of security and confidence she had never experienced before. She now had her own apartment and her own car. Things couldn't get any better! She drove around town showing off her new car. She made her first two payments but missed the third one. True to his word, her father took the car away from her and sold it. He wasn't being cruel or unfair. He just wanted to teach her a sense of responsibility. Art had given her a stern warning about what would happen if she failed to make the payments on her car. She had failed, and she was totally distraught by her predicament.

Polly decided to move to Minneapolis, find a job, and go to business school. She had been saving money for a long time. One thing she was good at was hoarding money. At the end of August, she bought a bus ticket and asked Ken to give her a ride to her parents' house so she could pick up some of her belongings and let her parents in on her plans. When she told her parents what she planned to do, they said, "Well, honey, if that's what you want, you have our blessing." Art and Lillian put on a brave front, but inside they were crying. Daddy's little girl was all grown up and had become a woman overnight.

That afternoon Polly and her friend Janis boarded the Greyhound bus headed for Minneapolis. Ken stood next to the bus waving at Polly, who was sitting next to the window waving back. Oh God, how he loved her. His eyes began to water and a tear rolled down his cheek. He got all choked up, and when he looked up, the bus was gone. He turned sadly and walked back to his car. His heart felt as if it had been ripped out of his chest. As he watched the bus disappear in the distance, he knew he would miss her desperately. Ken had loved Polly since they were in fifth grade. He had been so sure that they would one day be married, but when he proposed marriage to Polly, she tried to let him down easy telling him that she wanted to experience all that life had to offer before she settled down. Now the love of his life was gone

and he didn't know if he'd ever see her again. He
decided that now would be a good time to go to California. He wanted to see the ocean and maybe do
some surfing. Besides, it would be good to see how
the other half lived. A week after Polly moved to Minneapolis, Ken left for California.

CHAPTER 12

The bus ride to Minneapolis was over before they knew it. Minneapolis was much larger than they had anticipated. Polly and Janis had arrived during peak business hours and gotten caught up in the hustle and bustle of the people who crowded the sidewalks. They were bedazzled by the magnificence of the city. They hailed a cab and asked the driver if he would please take them to a nice hotel. The taxi driver took them to a hotel just a few blocks away. The room they rented was small but it would do. The noise of the city was music to their ears. The action in the city excited them. There was so much they wanted to see and do.

After the girls freshened up, they left the hotel and walked around town checking out the sights. They walked a few blocks up the street to a small restaurant on the corner. The place was packed with customers. Most of them were very young and seemed to know each other. They appeared to be a tightly knit group. They spoke much faster than most country folks and didn't have an accent. When Janis and

Polly walked in, the stares were obvious. Here were two gorgeous young women who dressed with class, and any normal male would have to be blind not to notice.

They sat in a booth, where a waitress handed them a menu. The waitress appeared to be in her early thirties, with shoulder length black hair and a pleasant disposition. Both girls decided to order cheeseburgers, fries, and strawberry shakes. They talked about how glad they were to be on their own and how anxious they were to be independent. They had many great memories of Pipestone that would forever be etched in their hearts, but they were glad to have left. Maybe someday they would go back to Pipestone, but for now they wanted to experience life in the big city. They had both led very sheltered lives and were ready for the excitement and fun that awaited them in Minneapolis.

When they were done eating, they paid the check and left the restaurant. Walking around town, they couldn't help but gawk at the huge buildings. They window-shopped and dreamed of all the beautiful clothes they planned to buy once they started working. Polly loved clothes, and had promised herself she would one day own the most chic and glamorous wardrobe money could buy. Sophistication was already part of Polly's character.

The next morning, they had breakfast at the same restaurant, and then set out to find the unemployment office. Polly got a job at the Singer Sewing Machine Company as a telephone operator. Polly's expectations of big city life had not fallen short. It was everything she dreamed it would be and more. She loved every minute of it. The corner restaurant became their hangout, where they met many new friends who were as young as they were. As it turned out, some of these young people had moved to Minneapolis from other cities in Minnesota looking for a more exciting life, just like Janis and Polly.

Polly met a young man named David. He was nineteen and very handsome. One of the nights when Janis and Polly were having dinner, David approached their table and introduced himself. He had dark brown hair, brown eyes, thick eyebrows, kissable lips, and a body to die for. He asked them if they would like to go to a party at one of his friend's apartments just down the street. The girls looked at each other and Polly said to Janis, "We've been here a week and haven't done anything fun." Polly looked at David and said, "Yes. We'd love to go." They finished their dinner, left the restaurant, and walked a few blocks down the street accompanied by the most divinely handsome man either girl had ever seen. There was a definite sexual attraction between Polly and David. She wanted him, and every time he smiled at her she felt butterflies in her stomach.

When they arrived at the hotel, they entered through a side door, climbed three flights of stairs, and walked down a small corridor till they reached the end. They heard music coming from one of the rooms. The room they entered was small but nicely decorated. There were a few young couples sitting on the chairs and the couch. The girls could see bottles of liquor being passed around. These people seemed to be respectable. David's friend Willie was twenty-one years old, with blonde hair and blue eyes. He was fairly handsome. David introduced Polly and Janis to the other people in the room. After the introductions, David asked Polly if she would care to dance. She said she would. He led her to the middle of the small room and pulled her close. Her body went limp as she melted into his arms. His touch made her body quiver. He kissed her gently on the lips, and when the dance was over, Polly was so weak in the knees it was all she could do to shakily make her way to the couch.

As Polly and David sat on the couch, they carried on a conversation as if they had known each other for a long time. This man was intelligent, knowledge-able, and assertive. To Polly, he seemed wise beyond his years. She hung on his every word. It was only now that she became aware of how sheltered she had been and how naïve she was. She had a burning desire to learn and experience all that life had to of-fer. When the party was over, David walked Polly and Janis back to their hotel and asked Polly if she would like to go out with him the following weekend. She said she would.

Later that night, as she lay in bed unable to fall asleep, David permeated her thoughts to the point where she could feel his presence. She was totally infatuated with him. Polly even thought she might just be in love with him, so powerful was the attrac-tion. She found it hard to believe that an innocent kiss could capture her heart so completely. At work the next day she found it difficult to concentrate on her job.

The week seemed to drag as she anticipated the coming weekend. After work, Polly and Janis went shopping for new clothes. The clothing stores in downtown Minneapolis were fabulous. They carried labels from Paris, Italy, and many other parts of the world. There were also fashions from New York on display in the shop windows. All the girls could do was look because they couldn't afford the prices. They would have to shop at the less expensive discount stores. Polly's two aunts had spoiled her when it came to fashion. They had traveled all over the world and always brought back some exquisite designs for Polly. If there was one thing Polly was an expert at, it was fashion.

Clothes were far more expensive in Minneapolis than in Pipestone. The few clothes she bought were nothing to brag about, but the girls were content with their modest purchases. On Friday after work, Polly rushed home. She ran the water in the tub, making sure there were plenty of bubbles. After she had soaked in the tub awhile, she lotioned every part of her body making sure her skin was not only clean, but sensuously soft. She meticulously applied her makeup and combed her hair, after which she sprayed on a fragrant perfume. The baby blue cotton skin-tight dress she wore accentuated the curves of her body. Her blonde hair and blue eyes made her appearance that much more attractive. She was now ready for the gorgeous man who would be picking her up.

Polly was a bit nervous, but Janis told her she looked beautiful and had nothing to worry about. David showed up right on time. Janis answered the door and invited him in. As he walked into the room, Janis got a whiff of his after-shave, which smelled so good it made her feel weak in the knees. He smelled so good and looked so devastatingly handsome it made Janis wish he had been her date. When David saw Polly, he told her how great she looked and asked if she was ready to go. She said she was and they left.

David was driving an old beat-up Buick four-door. As he drove west on Second Street, Polly asked him where they were going. With a sneaky smile he said, "You'll find out real soon." Polly said, "Okay, I'll let you surprise me. I'm sure whatever you've planned will be fine." She was smiling at him as he said, "Yes. I think you'll love what I have planned for us tonight."

He turned on South Dakota, and turning to Polly, asked, "You don't mind if I stop to pick up some friends, since they're going to the same party we are and need a ride?" She said it would be okay. He drove a few more blocks before he pulled up in front of a house that was painted dark gray and looked medieval – like something out of The Rocky Horror Picture Show. Polly got a queasy, uncomfortable feeling in the pit of her stomach. David asked her if she would like to go in for a minute. In her mind she was saying "No," but when she opened her mouth she said, "Yes".

They got out of the car and walked up some stairs. Polly kept thinking there was something about the house she didn't like. She felt like running, but against her better judgment she followed David. David knocked on the door a couple of times. A man in his early thirties answered the door and invited them in. They walked into a very large and messy room that looked more like a junkyard than a place where people actually lived. The man asked them to please sit down, which they did. This man was creepy-looking; he resembled a mummy. The uneasy feeling Polly had experienced when she saw the house escalated. The "mummy" said he would tell the rest of the guys that the company had arrived. He walked out of the room and down a dark, dreary hallway. As he walked, the floor made a squeaky sound.

As soon as he was gone, David grabbed Polly and kissed her forcefully on the mouth, not gently like before. She could sense that this was not the David she had become infatuated with. This one was crude and aggressive. He pulled her roughly against the sofa and began ripping off her dress. Polly started screaming hysterically, "Stop it David! What are you doing?" He completely ignored her screams and continued his assault. She continued screaming as loud as she could, but her screams only reverberated in the dusty old house. David spread her legs apart and penetrated her. The pain of his very large penis entering her was excruciating. Polly continued screaming as each thrust caused more pain. He moaned louder as he climaxed and lay panting on top of her.

When he got off her, Polly was relieved that the nightmare was over but, to her terror, it was about to get worse. When she opened her eyes, the "mummy" was standing over her with his huge penis in his hand, stroking it till it got hard. He warned her not to move or he would kill her. Polly was already weakened and dazed by the first attack. The "mummy" laid his filthy body on top of her, and again she felt excruciating pain as he entered her. As she was being brutally raped a second time, she looked up, and to her horror, Polly saw four more men waiting their turn, and there was nothing she could do to stop it. By the time the last man was through raping her, she had become numb from the indescribable pain these ugly, foul-smelling men had inflicted on her. She was in a state of shock and felt like throwing up. In her entire life, she had never been so frightened. The violence of the attacks she had been forced to endure had her left weak and light-headed. She was in the throes of a nightmare from which she could not awaken. Polly was sobbing uncontrollably and praying these vicious men would not kill her.

David approached her as she lay there sobbing, and threatened to kill her if she told anyone. He said in a malicious voice, "If you tell anyone about what just happened, you'll never see another sunrise. Do you understand what I'm telling you, bitch?" He back-handed her, rendering her almost unconscious. Polly screamed in terror, "Please don't hit me again! I promise not to say a word." David's threat increased her terror. She desperately wanted this unspeakable nightmare to be over. In her mind she kept praying to God, "Please, dear God, spare my life."

David told Polly to get dressed so he could take her back to her hotel. She looked at David and couldn't believe how badly she had misjudged him. The shock of the gang rape turned to anger, and all she could think about was how much she wanted to kill this bastard. She was also angry at herself for putting herself in such a precarious situation with a man she hardly knew.

She got back to the hotel at 10:00 p.m. Janis was out, so after locking the door, she walked into the room and broke down, sobbing hysterically. When she had no more tears left to shed, she walked into the bathroom, filled the tub with water, took off her tattered clothes, and got in. She was still in a lot of pain, and the thought of being so brutally violated both angered and disgusted her. She scrubbed her skin until it was raw. She could feel shock setting in again and began to panic. She had to keep telling herself that everything was going to be all right, but in her mind she was still screaming. She just wanted the pain to go away. Polly wanted desperately to tell someone about the rape, but David's threat echoed in her head. She knew he meant it, and it petrified her. At this moment, she wanted to die.

When she was done bathing, she gently dried herself with a towel. The physical pain of the assault was killing her. She put on her bathrobe, threw the clothes she had been wearing into a plastic bag, and hid them in the back of her closet with the intention of discarding them in the dumpster located at the back of the hotel. She slowly walked over to the bed and very carefully lay down. She closed her eyes and fell asleep almost immediately. In her sleep, she re-lived the horrendous nightmare of the degradation and violence she had endured that evening. She could actually smell the stench of the "mummy" as he lay on top of her. She woke up screaming hysterically. She was sweating, and her whole body was shaking uncontrollably.

She was alone in the darkness with only a ray of light shining through a small tear in the curtain. Polly felt as if she were losing her grip on reality. She found it hard to believe that she had been so gullible and naïve. She mulled over in her mind the events and circumstances that had led to this terrifying night. When she was finally able to fall asleep again, it was three o'clock in the morning. The same nightmare recurred over and over again as she slept.

Janis had returned from her night job to find Polly sleeping. When Polly awoke, the pain had subsided a little. She was glad that it was a weekend so she didn't have to go to work. She desperately wanted to talk to someone about her ordeal, but she knew David would follow through on his threat. Having no other choice, she would have to suffer in silence and carry the burden all by herself.

As time passed, she began to feel a little more confidence in herself. Her life had been turned up-side down, and even though she was still an emo-tional wreck, she revisited the restaurant where she had first met David. She didn't think he would be stupid enough to show his face at that restaurant again. He and his friends were probably searching out their next victim.

Polly hadn't eaten very well in the past few days, so she stuffed herself until she couldn't eat another bite. That night she slept better than she had in quite a while. The following day when she returned to her job, she immersed herself in her work in an effort to retain her sanity.

CHAPTER 13

One day after work as she was walking by a dance studio, Polly saw a sign that read "Dance Instructor Wanted". She walked in and asked to see the boss. The owner was an extremely handsome man in his mid-thirties with blonde hair and the muscular body of a dancer. He asked Polly if he could be of some assistance. She politely answered, "Yes, sir. I noticed your sign on the window advertising for a dance instructor." He asked her if she knew anything about dancing. She told him that she loved to dance and had been dancing all her life but had no professional experience. The owner said, "Well, let me see your stuff." He walked over to the record booth, where he put an album on the record player. He took Polly by the hand and led her to the center of the dance floor. They began to dance, and she gracefully and fluidly followed his every move. He was so impressed by her natural talent that he hired her on the spot. Polly knew all the dance steps and was not only an excellent dancer, but she was also very personable. She loved being around people.

In the evenings Polly could now do the thing she loved most and get paid for it without giving up her other job. On her first night, she danced with older men who were very light on their feet as they glided across the floor. She dressed elegantly, and at eighteen she was a sight to behold. In just a matter of days, she became the most popular dance instructor. Many of the older men waited their turn to dance with Polly. Some of them would ask her out to dinner, and on occasion she would accept their invitation. Polly was a good listener, and learned a lot just by listening to her more mature male students. They would talk and she would absorb the wisdom they were willing to impart. She had made one horrendous mistake, which she was adamantly determined never to make again.

During the weekend, she loved going home on the bus to visit her family and friends. She would regale them with stories about life in the big city. The one thing she was careful not to divulge was the sadistic gang rape she had endured, not even to her mother. There were times when her secret ate at her insides.

Once when Polly was home, she went to a party. All her friends were there and very glad to see her again. They wanted to know what big city life was like, so she told them. They were very impressed with all she said. Her brother asked her how life was treating her. She lied and told him everything was fine. Art's friend Bob had his eye on Polly. She found him quite handsome. Bob was six feet tall with dark brown hair and a slender build. He was also a fabulous dresser. When they were alone, he asked Polly if she would mind if he stopped by to see her the next time he was in Minneapolis. She said, "Sure. Why not?"

She didn't see a problem with it, so she gave Bob her address.

On Monday, when she returned to Minneapolis, she registered for the fall semester at a small business college. Going to school and working two jobs kept her very busy. Every weekend she would add a new pair of shoes and a new dress to her wardrobe.

A week after school started, Janis moved back to South Dakota with her husband to give their marriage another try. Her husband came from a very wealthy family. Janis and her husband had met in high school and had fallen madly in love. They were married in their senior year, only to split up six months later due to irreconcilable differences. That's when Polly had invited Janis to move with her to Minneapolis. Janis and Polly had been very close friends since they were in kindergarten. They had also been members of the Thirteen Nifty Teens. Polly would now have to look for a new roommate.

While attending business college, Polly met a girl named Lenora who was looking for someone to room with. The following day Polly asked Lenora if she would like to room with her. Lenora eagerly agreed. She only had a couple of suitcases, so she moved in that very day. The two girls had dinner at the neighborhood restaurant, and as they talked, it didn't take them long to discover they had a lot in common. They became the best of friends. Janis and Polly hadn't had much in common even though they had been lifelong friends. Lenora loved clothes as much as Polly did. Whenever Polly bought a pair of new shoes, Lenora would go out and buy an identical pair. They were both very fashion- conscious, and at times seemed to be in competition when it came to making a fashion statement. They would double date guys they felt they could trust.

One afternoon, Polly needed to go into the heart of the city because she had taken on another part-time job at a small restaurant. She rode the trolley car and hung on for dear life every time it rounded a corner. The trolley car had traveled a few blocks before Polly finally got a seat. After approximately 40 blocks, Polly stood up. A man sitting next to her stood too. Polly found his behavior quite peculiar. She sat back down immediately, and the strange man sat down too. After the trolley had traveled a couple more blocks, Polly needed to get off, so she stood up once more, and the man did the same. This scared the hell out of her, so as soon as the trolley came to a halt, she exited. The man got off as well.

Polly's mind started racing as she became more and more frightened. She began walking faster, but the man kept at her heels. She wanted to run, but she was wearing four-inch high-heeled shoes. She was walking as fast as she could and praying silently for God's help. Polly was becoming really frantic. She turned back to see if he was following her, and how close he was. He was practically on top of her, and he was breathing heavily. She wondered how many other lunatics were running loose in Minneapolis. Her destination was still a block away. Most of the buildings were at least twenty stories high. Dark shadows filled the streets, serving to make her dilemma much more intense. The hairs at the back of her neck were standing on end. Suddenly, she felt a hand grab her. She screamed in terror as she turned to look at her attacker. Her sudden jerk made him lose his grip on her, and he fell onto the sidewalk. He grabbed her leg, and wouldn't let go. Polly asked, "Please, mister, what the hell do you want from me? Just leave me alone."

She managed to pull her leg away from his grip and take a few steps back. He looked up at her and said, "I don't want to hurt you. I just want to go out with you." Polly looked down at this pervert and said, "Mister, that's one hell of a way to ask a person out on a date." He told Polly he was sorry and would never try that again. She turned and walked away, leaving him lying on the sidewalk. She couldn't believe how many crazy people were wandering the streets. She was beside herself. She promised herself she would never go anywhere by herself again.

She was ten minutes late to work. She needed this part-time job just to survive. The restaurant was owned by an elderly couple whose love for each other seemed genuine. Polly's new job was as a hostess, overseeing the banquet and taking reservations. Most of the clientele were a little more sophisticated than some of the people she had met thus far. She loved being around all this refinement and sophistication. Working three jobs and going to school was difficult, but she had no other choice. She now recognized the high price she had to pay for the independence she valued.

Her favorite job was the one she had at the dance studio. She loved being around men. For her, dancing was more recreation than work. Sometimes when she was dancing, she would reminisce about the good times she had had when she was in high school and wished she could turn back the clock. She would remember all the dances she had attended with her friends, whom she missed more than anything. She also thought about Ken and wondered what he was doing. Polly was feeling the loneliness that came from being on her own.

On the weekend, she took the bus home to visit her family and friends. When she arrived, she discovered that her brother's friend Bob was there. There was a definite attraction between them. Bob asked her out and she accepted. When he went to pick her up, Polly looked just as beautiful as she always did. For the first time since the rape, she was feeling more at ease. She trusted Bob; besides, she knew if he tried anything her brother would kick his butt. Polly was a passionate person and needed to be loved. She couldn't allow the rape to deter her from finding the love she so desperately needed.

Polly and Bob toured around Pipestone as she recalled all the wonderful times she had enjoyed growing up in this small Minnesota town. She would forever cherish those memories. Pipestone had grown into a beautiful town. The credit went to the City Fathers, who had the vision and fortitude to nurture its growth. Skeptics said Pipestone would fail because it was so isolated, but the City Fathers held fast to their dream. Pipestone was now nestled amidst one of the largest agricultural meccas in the northern plains. It had continued to thrive, and its citizens were very proud to be a part of this wonderful little community.

Bob and Polly attended a couple of parties that evening. Polly loved that Bob was such a great listener. He was also a perfect gentleman. They drove out to the Three Maidens. They looked into each other's eyes and saw the passion. As they kissed, Polly felt herself melting into Bob's arms. She liked the feeling and didn't want the moment to end. The touch of his lips made her body quiver. He whispered in her ear, "Let me make love to you." She said "Yes" without hesitation. As their lovemaking climaxed, Polly screamed in ecstasy. For the first time in her life she felt like a woman. Bob had been gentle and loving, making her feel special and desirable. She was convinced that Bob was the man for her.

When she returned to Minneapolis, all she could think about was Bob. At work, he was constantly on her mind. She was anxious to see him again. When she got home that night, her roommate Lenora told her that there were two cowboys downstairs waiting to see her. Polly screamed and ran out the door. She ran down the hallway wondering how in the world those Texas cowboys discovered where she lived. Lenora followed her into the hallway and told Polly she was just kidding. Polly turned and gave Lenora a dirty look as she said, "You scared the hell out of me. I really thought those cowboys had found out where I lived." Polly and Laura had had fun with them in Texas, but wanted nothing to do with them in Minneapolis. After Polly's fright subsided, she and Lenora laughed till they cried.

The two girls enjoyed each other's company so much. They had bonded like sisters. Polly didn't have a sister, but if she had, she would want her to be just like Lenora.

At 7:00 p.m., Polly reported to the dance studio for her scheduled appointments. The men she was teaching to dance were much older than she. One of her clients, Mr. Mormon, had been taking dancing lessons for over twenty years. It was his way of breaking the monotony of his boring life. At the age of eighty, he had been alone for over two decades. His beloved Margaret had died, and he found himself at a loss. Polly filled the void by being his friend.

After class that night, Polly and Mr. Mormon went to a restaurant down the street from the dance studio. He told her about his life as a schoolteacher and the many wonderful years he spent with Margaret, who had also been a schoolteacher. They had four boys who were now married and living in different places across the United States. He was alone. Throughout the years he had had affairs with different women. Some of them even wanted to marry him, but he told Polly he would never marry again. Margaret would always be the love of his life, and he longed for the day when he would see her lovely face again.

Polly got home at midnight totally exhausted. She was so tired that when she finally went to bed, she tossed and turned. She kept thinking about Bob. He had told her that he would visit her during the week. The thought excited her as she remembered the way he had made love to her. For the next few days, Polly daydreamed about Bob. She wanted him to make love to her again. In class the following day, she couldn't concentrate on her lessons.

Bob finally showed up on Wednesday, and when Polly answered the door, her eyes lit up at the sight of him. They smiled at each other and exchanged pleasantries. There was something special about this man. He was kind, generous, and a perfect lover. What more could a woman ask for? Polly couldn't be happier. Bob asked if she wanted to go out to dinner and then maybe take in a movie. Polly said whatever he wanted to do was fine with her.

Polly decided to wear something dressy. They decided to eat at one of the restaurants in downtown Minneapolis. When they arrived at the restaurant, Bob got out of the car and opened the door for Polly. They entered holding hands. The attraction between them was electrifying. It was apparent that they were falling in love with each other. Bob and Polly dined in one of the more exclusive restaurants. The maitre d' wore a black tuxedo and a red bow tie, and was quite distinguished-looking.

As they ate, they kept making eye contact. The meal was superb, as was the service. After dinner, they walked to a movie theater located a few blocks down the street. The theater resembled an old Greek theater, with ceilings at least forty-five feet high and intricately carved columns. The design was absolutely beautiful. The theater was showing "Gone with the Wind". It was the most romantic movie Polly had ever seen. The cinematography and the acoustics made her feel as if she were actually one of the characters. Both Bob and Polly enjoyed the movie immensely and were quite moved by the story line of the movie. Clark Gable and Vivien Leigh were incredible.

"Gone with the Wind" had put both Polly and Bob in a very romantic mood. They ended up making love till dawn and were reluctant to part company, but Polly had to attend school and go to work at the dance studio. They made love one last time, showered together, and ate breakfast at the diner down the street from Polly's before they finally parted. Polly went to class and Bob went back to Pipestone.

In the days that followed, Polly was immersed in the fast pace of city life. Lenora and Polly moved into a bigger house, which they shared with five other classmates. The house was on Pilsbury Street near the college. It was a six-bedroom, two-story, old Victorian house. The living arrangements were perfect. A family lived in two of the bedrooms, and the girls shared the other four bedrooms. They all shared the same kitchen. The living arrangements were also very economical and gave the girls the opportunity to save some money. It was also quite convenient because it was closer to town, where the action was.

Polly loved big city life. She loved the sounds, the sights, and even the smells. Even the sounds of the jackhammer pounding the cement and the ambulance sirens added to the excitement. The city was alive twenty-four hours a day. Once in a while the girls from the college would sneak into a nightclub and go dancing. They never failed to find partners to dance with, and if they were so inclined, they would leave with someone they had met at the bar, which meant they would probably get lucky.

Having missed her menstrual period for a couple of months, Polly became very apprehensive. She had never missed a period before. She wondered what the hell she was going to do if she was pregnant. When she saw Bob the following weekend in Pipestone, she told him there was a possibility that she might be pregnant. Bob held her and told her not to worry because if she did turn out to be pregnant he would marry her. He promised he would be a good husband and a good father to their child.

Polly appreciated his noble gesture and caring attitude, but she had already decided that if she was pregnant she would get an abortion. She felt she was too young for the responsibilities of motherhood. She explained to Bob how she felt and what she was planning to do. Bob pleaded with her saying, "Please, Polly, don't do it! We'll get married and everything will be okay." Polly was adamant about her decision and refused to be dissuaded. She reiterated that she was not ready to be a wife and mother. Bob's eyes teared-up as he told Polly that what she was planning was wrong. He tried desperately to convince her to have the baby, but Polly wouldn't budge. She was stubborn. Once her mind was made up, there was no changing it.

Polly asked Bob if he would be willing to help with the cost of the abortion. He said he had no money but was willing to sell his phonograph and give her the proceeds. Polly informed her parents about her pregnancy and her decision to get an abortion. They told her they would stand by her no matter what. Polly and her mother cried. She hated the thought of killing her unborn child, and the guilt weighed heavy in her heart.

When she returned to Minneapolis, she made an appointment to have the abortion done that very week. Lenora accompanied her to the doctor's office the day she was scheduled to have the abortion. Polly was terrified and feeling apprehensive about the whole thing. The procedure was over in twenty minutes. She felt nothing more than a little discomfort. She was relieved that her apprehensions had been unfounded. Physically she was okay, but the enormity of what she had just done weighed heavily upon her. She had just killed her unborn child!

When Polly got home, she went into her room to lie down. She felt weak and just wanted to sleep. Maybe in sleep the emotional pain would go away, but sleep eluded her. She tossed and turned until she fell into a semi-sleep. In this state, she could hear the far away cry of a baby. She dreamed that Bob was crying and pleading with her not to have the abortion. The words she told him during their last meeting echoed in her dream: "I'm too young; it'll ruin my life."

When Polly woke up, it was three o'clock in the morning. She had broken out in a cold sweat. Her heart was racing. Guilt was haunting her. None of her other friends knew what she had done. Polly was so depressed that she decided to stay home from class that day. She had no appetite and she didn't want to see anyone. She tried drinking a 7-Up to settle her stomach but it only made her more nauseous. For the next few days, Polly kept to herself. She had an empty feeling inside, as if her soul had been ripped out.

During the middle of the week, Bob came to visit. When she saw him, her eyes lit up and she smiled. It was the first time since her abortion that she felt like smiling. Bob's visit was well timed. His presence comforted her, and she knew his concern for her was genuine. He bought her roses and a box of cherry candy. She kissed him gently and thanked him for being so solicitous.

Bob was crazy about Polly and told her he still loved her and wanted to marry her. Polly told him she didn't want to marry anyone till she was twenty-one. As much as he loved her, Bob knew he was not the man for Polly. Before he left, he told her he loved her, but under the circumstances, felt it best if he didn't see her again. On his way out of Minneapolis, he stopped at the first bar he saw and got sloshed. He was so drunk that the other patrons in the bar couldn't quite make out what he was saying. The only intelligible words were "Polly. Beloved Polly." As he sat in the bar he kept reliving the times they had made love and all those romantic moments they had shared.

He passed out in the back seat of his car for a couple of hours. When he woke up, he was nearly freezing to death. It was the middle of January 1948. He hadn't realized it had been snowing all night, and there were at least four inches of snow on top of his car. When he finally cleaned the snow away, he drove very slowly back to Pipestone. He was suffering from the most horrible hangover he had ever experienced, and he promised himself he would never drink again. He knew it would be a long time before he would get over Polly.

CHAPTER 14

The winter of 1948 arrived with a vengeance in Minnesota. Some of the temperatures fell to forty below zero. Pipestone was cold, but all the concrete made Minneapolis feel a lot colder. As Polly walked to class with all her friends, they continually complained about the extremely cold weather. That very day, Polly bought herself a new fur coat. She hated the cold. She looked forward to the day when she could move to a warmer climate.

The howling winds echoed among the tall buildings. The snowdrifts that accumulated in the alleyways were at least four feet high. The walkways and the streets became so slick they resembled an ice skating rink. They were so slippery that if you weren't careful, you'd end up on your butt. The winter was so dismal, even the economy suffered. As beautiful as the summers were in Minnesota, the winters were unbearably harsh. During the winter months, everything seemed to come to a grinding halt.

Polly still suffered from the emotional devastation of her abortion. She continued working three jobs and going to class. Being without Bob left her feeling lonely and forlorn, but deep inside she knew she had made the right decision. She wasn't ready for marriage. Polly knew she had lost Bob and would probably never see him again. But she needed a man in her life. At a bar she and her friends frequented, she met a man named Pete. He was twenty-one years old with dark brown hair, brown eyes, bushy eye-brows, and a great personality. He was really quite handsome, and always seemed to be smiling. Pete liked to kid around, and once he got started you couldn't shut him up. His light-hearted attitude was actually his most endearing quality. The fact that he was a wonderful dancer attracted Polly.

Pete appeared very refined and well educated. He was also a stylish dresser. When he asked Polly if she'd go out with him, she told him she'd have to think about it and would let him know the next time she saw him. After all, she didn't want to appear too eager. Besides, after what she had just been through with Bob, she felt the need to be cautious about get-ting into a new relationship. Polly was no longer the naïve, carefree girl she had been when she arrived in Minneapolis. She had made some gigantic mistakes since she moved to the big city. Her mistakes had cost her dearly. She still suffered from the trauma of her brutal and violent rape, and as if that weren't enough, now she was suffering from the trauma of her abortion. She spent many sleepless nights feel-ing hopeless and very much alone. Polly knew she couldn't undo the past, but she also knew that her indomitable spirit would get her through these try-ing times.

Not being one to stay home moping, Polly partied with her friends on weekends. These wild parties in-cluded drinking, smoking, and promiscuity. One night during a dance lesson, her client was a charming young man named Ziggy who was in his early thirties and always gave Polly a generous tip. That evening, when Polly was ready to leave, he offered to give her a ride home. Ziggy owned a brand new yellow Lincoln. Polly was impressed because she had never seen such a fabulous car. It had electric windows and a radio. As Ziggy was driving Polly home, she became fascinated with the electric windows and kept opening and closing them. After a while Ziggy said, "Hey, do you want to break the windows?" She said "No", and thought, 'This guy's really touchy about his car.' Polly told him she had never been in a car with electric windows. Ziggy told her to take it easy, but she couldn't resist pushing the button a couple more times.

When she was through playing with the windows, she told him she was quite impressed with his car. He thanked her and asked if she was hungry. Polly told him she was famished, since she hadn't had anything to eat all day. Her stomach was growling and making funny noises. He drove down the street, made a left on Upton Street, and drove to a local burger joint. It was a fast food drive-in where the carhops wore roller skates and outfits that showed off their cute curves.

It was now spring in Minneapolis, and people could be seen strolling hand in hand on the sidewalks, walking their dogs, or jogging. The paralysis of winter was over, and the city was alive once more with activity. Ziggy and Polly ordered hamburgers, French fries, and cherry cokes. As he drove Polly home, Ziggy asked if she would like to have dinner with him. She said, "Yes."

The following evening, after Polly had given her last dance lesson, she and Ziggy dined at a very exclusive restaurant. He turned out to be a penny pincher who constantly complained about everything from the service to the food. There was no way she was going to date a nit-picking miser, and she decided she would not go out with Ziggy again. The next time he asked her out, she told him she was busy. She went as far as hiding in a closet when he came looking for her. Eventually he got the hint.

Polly and her friends attended a classy party that included business executives, high profile entrepreneurs, and several city politicians. The girls mingled with the guests and toured the huge house where the party was being held. As they walked around eavesdropping on conversations, they could hear people exaggerating their net worth and boasting about their supposedly prestigious accomplishments. Polly had never witnessed so many pretentious people gathered in one place. The house belonged to a prominent attorney for a big local firm. He was a bachelor and had the reputation of being quite a ladies' man. He was surrounded by several women who hung on his every word and vied for his attention.

When Polly and her friends entered the main parlor, they encountered a similar gathering of highly educated, prominent guests. Polly was not in the least bit intimidated. She looked lovely and felt quite confident even in the midst of these so-called social elites. A young man who was standing next to the credenza that was located near the fireplace was eyeing Polly. She felt someone staring at her, and as she turned around their eyes met. She smiled at him as he made his way through the crowd to where she was standing. The closer he got, the better he looked. Her heart was pounding as he approached her. He introduced himself, saying, "Hello. My name is Gene." Polly told him, "My name is Paulyn Hofelman." He shook her hand and told her he was pleased to meet her. His touch was electrifying.

Gene asked her if she was from Minneapolis, and she replied, "No. I'm originally from Pipestone. It's a very small town in the western part of the state." He told her it sounded quaint and most interesting. She responded, "It's okay, if you like small towns." He asked her what she was doing in Minneapolis. Polly told him she was working and going to school. Polly asked what he did for a living. He told her he was an airline pilot. He explained that he had been a fighter pilot during World War II, and had been highly decorated for his bravery during the bomb runs over Germany, but he really didn't like talking about it. He asked her if she would like to join him on the veranda. She said she'd love to. He got a couple of glasses of wine from the bar and they walked out to the veranda.

He sat next to Polly and handed her a glass of wine. He then proposed a toast to their new friendship, which he hoped would last a long time. From where they were sitting, they could hear the sounds of soft music and could see couples dancing. When they finished their glasses of wine, he asked Polly if she would like to dance. She said "Yes", and they walked hand in hand into the dimly lit room. Gene put his arm around Polly's waist, and as they began to dance he held her close. He commented on what an excellent dancer she was. She told him she was a dance instructor at a local dance studio.

As they continued to dance, Gene held her closer and kissed her on the lips. The not-so-gentle kiss excited her. When the party was over, he took her home and kissed her again. They found themselves mutually attracted to each other. As they said good night, a little voice inside told her this was the man with whom she wanted to spend the rest of her life. She found herself intrigued and fascinated by this charming, handsome man. When she went to bed that night, she could see his face every time she closed her eyes.

Gene and Polly began dating each other exclusively. They were almost inseparable. He drove her to her classes, to her jobs, and at the end of the day he drove her home. He was a gentle and romantic lover. So many things had gone wrong since she left Pipestone, she felt very fortunate to have met a man like Gene at such a low point in her life. He was gentle, kind, and undemanding.

Polly decided to let Gene accompany her to Pipestone on her next visit so she could introduce him to her family. They treated him very cordially until Lillian discovered his age. When Gene was out of earshot, she went through the roof and wanted to know why Polly would date a man that much older than her. She explained to her mom that he was a wonderful man with many endearing qualities, and she felt she was falling in love with him. Lillian closed her ears and her mind. As far as she was concerned, Gene was too old for Polly. End of discussion. She stormed out of the room.

Art gave Gene a tour of the ranch. He was very proud of all that he had accomplished. He had a big spread with lots of cattle and some of the finest steers in all of western Minnesota. When the tour was over, Art and Gene walked back to the house. As they walked in the door, they could sense something was wrong. She rushed over to Gene and said, "Let's get out of here. I want to go back to Minneapolis." She was very agitated. Gene asked her what was wrong. She told him she would fill him in later. Polly walked over and hugged her father and told him she and

Gene were going back to Minneapolis. Her father wanted to know why they were leaving so soon. Polly told him she had to go back to work the following day.

As Polly and Gene were driving back to Minneapolis, she told him that her mother did not approve of their relationship. She said, "My mother thinks you're too old for me. She feels I should be dating men closer to my own age." He replied, "Maybe once she gets to know me, she'll have a change of heart." Polly said, "I know my mother. Once she makes up her mind, she won't budge." Gene asked, "What do you think we should do?" Polly answered, "I know one thing for sure, I'm not giving you up no matter what anybody thinks. I love you too much to let you go." Gene told her he loved her too.

When they arrived in Minneapolis they drove straight to his apartment, where they spent the remainder of the weekend making love. They couldn't get enough of each other. What started out as a disastrous weekend ended up being a superbly romantic one. Instead of splitting them up, Lillian's remarks only served to bring Polly and Gene closer together.

The following weekend, they drove out to Sunrise Lake to do a little fishing. It was reputed to be one of the best fishing places in the world. It was well stocked, and native bass were plentiful. Polly and Gene went fishing every chance they got. The area was so peaceful. At night they camped under the stars, with a full moon dispelling the darkness. Nothing could be more romantic than making love under a star-filled sky surrounded by the sounds of nature and no human intrusion for miles and miles.

In Minneapolis, they attended almost every Minnesota Twins home game. The Twins were having an excellent season. The 1948-49 team was one of the best the Twins had had in many years. They were proud of their team. The stands were always filled with cheering fans. The Twins were victorious most of the time. After the game, everyone would go dancing at Snyder's Bar. When Polly and Gene danced, they were the envy of the bar because they were both very good dancers.

Whenever Polly and Gene were together, there was never a boring moment. For the first time in her life Polly felt complete. Gene was totally in love with Polly and asked her to marry him. She accepted his proposal, and even though no specific date had been set, they were now officially engaged.

The following weekend, Polly took the bus home, hoping her parents had changed their minds about Gene. Unfortunately, they stood fast in their opinion that Gene was much too old for her. She told them that he had proposed marriage and she had accepted. The wedding would be some time in the summer. Her parents were adamantly opposed to the marriage, and told her that she could go ahead and marry him but it would be without their consent.

That entire weekend Polly was deeply depressed. As she lay in bed surrounded by darkness, she cried herself to sleep. She missed Gene very much, and wished with all her heart that her parents would accept him, but she knew it would never happen. Ultimately, her love for her parents and her desire for their approval outweighed her love for Gene, and she decided not to go through with the wedding.

On Saturday, she went to see some of her friends. She'd been gone from Pipestone for almost a year. Nothing seemed to have changed during the time she had been gone. A lot of her friends seemed content living in Pipestone. Polly, however, wasn't ready to return to Pipestone permanently.

Upon her return to Minneapolis, she called Gene and asked him to pick her up. When she saw Gene, she didn't have the heart to tell him she had decided to break off their relationship. She knew it would break his heart, so she decided to say nothing. They continued dating. Knowing how her parents felt about Gene, Polly never mentioned his name to them again. Gene and Polly continued seeing each other despite her parents' objections. There was something intoxicating about this man, and the more she saw of him, the deeper in love Polly became.

CHAPTER 15

During the summer of 1949, Pipestone held "The Song of Hiawatha Pageant" to celebrate the Indian traditions. The citizens of Pipestone respected the Indian way of life, and the Pageant was their way of expressing their respect. The celebration included a depiction of the sacred way of life around the quarries.

In the 1930's the Indian School put on performances of "The Song of Hiawatha". Most of the children who performed were from the Indian School. The first productions were held near the Three Maidens, but due to the lack of rain, the creek finally dried up. The school was shut down and the production was discontinued. It wasn't until 1949 that the people of Pipestone took an interest in bringing back the Pageant.

Robert S. Owens had always had the desire to produce the show. He purchased the perfect spot for the enactment of this drama. The land belonged to R. L. Palmer. It had been a long time since the production had been discontinued, and a lot of vigorous work went into putting on the first performance. The entire community became involved. The various businesses offered their services. Many of the performers were local white people from Pipestone. To the dismay of the community, the first performance was rained out, but on the bright side, the lake now had plenty of water. Teepees were erected around the lake, and thanks to the rain, canoes could be used to depict the way Indian families had lived at the turn of the century before the white man came along. Because of the tireless and unified efforts of the Pipestone community, the audience witnessed how the blood of the Indians had flowed. "The Song of Hiawatha" would forever remain etched in the minds of all the people who had the privilege of seeing this wonderful and memorable production.

Polly continued her weekend visits to her parents, but never took Gene to her parents' home again. Even though she was madly in love with Gene, her weekly trips to Pipestone were her way of keeping in touch with her family and friends. During one of her weekend visits, her father told her that rather than make the trip home every weekend, she should just move back home. He said there was a position open at the bank and she should apply for it. He also told her he would talk to Mr. Jennings, the bank president, about hiring her. Polly said she would think about it and let him know the following weekend.

During the bus ride back to Minneapolis, she thought about her father's suggestion, and seriously considered his offer to intervene on her behalf for the job opening. What her father said made a lot of sense. She had been in Minneapolis just a little over two years, and had experienced a lifestyle she could never have known had she remained in Pipestone. She had many fond memories of her life in Minneapolis, but she also had some horrifying ones. She didn't care much for school, so quitting would be no big deal. By the time she arrived in Minneapolis, Polly had made her decision.

When she arrived at her apartment, she told Lenore that she had decided to move back home. Lenore was completely caught off guard. Polly had been her best friend for the past two years. Tears filled her eyes as she embraced Polly and told her how desperately she would miss her. Both girls started crying.

Gene came by that evening to take Polly out to dinner. She told him that she was moving back to Pipestone and would be giving her employers notice. She also told him she was quitting school. Gene was devastated by Polly's announcement of her plans. That night after dinner, he took her to his apartment and made love to her all night. Gene was a magnificent lover.

As Polly lay in his arms, her desire to marry this man was overwhelming, but she knew her parents would never approve of their relationship. She knew without question that this was the man for her. Polly told Gene she wanted to continue seeing him, but because of her parents' disapproval of their relationship they would have to be very discreet. He told her he loved her so much that he would willingly make the trip to Pipestone just to be with her.

The following Friday, with a heavy heart, Polly took the bus back to Pipestone, even though she was having second thoughts about her decision to move back home. She was devastated at having to leave the man she loved. Since they had first met, their time together had been exciting and romantic. The memory of their indescribably sensual lovemaking made her departure that much more difficult.

She had a window seat on the bus, and as the bus left Minneapolis, Polly stared out the window lost in thought. She felt an emptiness and desperation that was devastating. As the bus traveled towards Pipestone, Polly's greatest hope was that her stay in Pipestone would not become permanent. The past two years had flown by so quickly. She found it hard to believe that her naïveté and bad judgment had resulted in the rape that left her so badly scarred both mentally and emotionally. Life in Minneapolis hadn't been all bad, but at this point in her life, she felt the need to return home and reevaluate her life. Tears streamed down her face, and she felt very much alone.

There was a part of Polly that was distraught at leaving Minneapolis. She was no longer the naïve young girl who had left Pipestone in search of new adventures. In the two years since she had left home, she felt she had grown into a more mature and discreet woman. Even her self-confidence had grown tremendously. Despite her desire to remain in Minneapolis, Polly had become homesick, and she felt a nagging need to be with her family and friends. She missed them! Pipestone might be a small hick town, but she loved it. It was her home, and she carried all the wonderful memories of her life in Pipestone buried in her heart.

Polly was not a very religious person, but she had done things in Minneapolis about which she felt very ashamed, even though she had no regrets. Contemplating the course her life would take now that she was returning to Pipestone made the bus ride seem endless. She could only hope that the change in lifestyle she was making would be for the better.

As the bus pulled into Pipestone, she could see her parents waiting for her. There was a part of her that was glad and relieved to be home. She learned that she had gotten the job at the bank, thanks to her father's intervention. She was to report to work on Monday.

CHAPTER 16

Her first weekend home Polly attended a party. She saw a multitude of familiar faces. Most of her high school friends and acquaintances were there. She ran into Emily Ann. They were both very glad to see each other again. As they reminisced about their high school days, they noticed that most of the members of the Thirteen Nifty Teens were also at the party. Little by little, the TNTs began to converge and form a huddle just like when they were in high school. Before long they were all reminiscing about old times and laughing at all the silly things they had done. They had known each other since they were in grade school. All the girls told Polly how glad they were that she was back, because things just hadn't been the same since she'd been gone.

Some of the guys, like Jack, Jimmy, and Dale, showed up at the party. Since a party wasn't a party without booze, they brought their own supply. Dale was the most handsome of the group, and Polly spotted him right away. He glanced at her and smiled. She smiled back. Dale happened to be Donna's brother. Donna was one of the Thirteen Nifty Teens. Even though he and Polly had crossed paths a thousand times during their high school days, she had never taken an interest in him.

The girls stood around swapping stories of their lives during the past two years. Polly's was the most incredible of all. They all wanted to know more about life in Minneapolis. Polly regaled them with stories about all the good-looking men she had dated, but was very careful not to mention the bad things that had happened to her. She kept those horrifying experiences to herself. These memories were still very painful, and she was determined to bury them deep within herself.

During the course of the party, Dale walked over and offered Polly a beer, which she gladly accepted. She chugged it down – partly to show off and partly to show the guys that she could drink as much as they could. Dale noticed that she could match the guys drink for drink, and he was quite impressed. Most of the girls he had partied with couldn't drink as much as he did, and if the truth be told, he drank a lot. Dale liked to drink. He had started drinking at the age of thirteen when he hung around some of the older guys in Pipestone. Some of the town drunks would sneak liquor for him from the basement bar at the Calumet Hotel, and he and his friend Jimmy would get drunk on one bottle of beer. As the years progressed his tolerance for alcohol grew, as did his drinking capacity. He had the reputation of being a party animal. He could care less what people said about him.

Dale and Polly became quite drunk as they chugged one beer after another. They were having a contest to see who would pass out first. Neither one yielded. Finally, when they were both about to pass out, they quit.

Jimmy, Donna, Dale, and Polly left the party so drunk that they were trying to hold each other up. As they were driving back to the ranch, they got a flat tire but were too drunk to change it. Their speech was slurred and they swayed when they stood up. Dale asked Jimmy, "Who's going to change the tire?" Jimmy retorted, "Maybe we can try changing it together. You think?" It took both of them half an hour to change the tire, and the whole time Dale kept telling Polly how cute she was and how he thought he was falling in love with her. Polly just took it all in. She loved flattery.

When Dale finally got Polly home he gave her an innocent goodnight kiss. She had been caught off guard, and when she entered the house, she couldn't decipher what she was feeling. She had been unexpectedly charmed by Dale's sweet talk and flattery. Polly was in love with Gene, yet Dale's suave charm had unsettled her feelings. She knew she had a big dilemma on her hands!

The following day, Dale called and asked if she would like to go cruising with him. She said she would have to clear it with her parents but didn't think there would be a problem. She told Dale the only reason she felt compelled to get her parents' permission was because she respected them and the fact that she was now living under their roof. He told her he understood and would call her back later.

Dale picked Polly up at 7:00 p.m. that evening, and they went cruising all over Pipestone. They drove to Hatfield and went dancing at the Hollyse Hawk Ballroom. Polly didn't even know if Dale could dance, but to her amazement he turned out to be a great dancer. He could really jitterbug. If he was trying to impress Polly, he had certainly succeeded. She was totally impressed! She loved being with Dale because he was so much fun to be with. He had one flaw that was a turn-off for Polly: he drank too much. She loved to party, and she didn't mind getting drunk once in a while, but it wasn't something she wanted to do on a daily basis.

On Monday, she began her job at the bank. Everyone seemed very friendly as they welcomed her on her first day. She knew most of the people who worked at the bank, but not on a personal basis. Mrs. Wells was the head teller in charge of operations. Polly would be training on-the-job for a few days under her supervision. Until she learned the more intricate facets of banking, she would be a gofer, fetching things and doing miscellaneous jobs. She didn't mind because she was eager to learn the banking business. She loved working with money, and hoped to have lots of money herself someday.

Ever since Polly was young, she had learned to deposit her money in a bank savings account. She liked watching her savings grow. It gave her a great deal of satisfaction. Her father had taught her to save money for a "rainy day". He had told her, "You never know when an emergency might occur." Polly had never liked the idea of being broke.

Polly's greatest asset was her ability to deal with people. She was definitely a "people person". She was also a fast learner. Within a few days she had mastered the teller business. All of the bank officers as well as the bank president were quite impressed with her ability to grasp things so quickly. She was always very courteous to the customers.

After her abhorrent experiences in Minneapolis, her life was finally on track. The one thing she missed in Minneapolis was her beloved Gene. Because of her parents' disapproval, she was apprehensive about her relationship with him. She dreaded the thought that she would eventually have to end it with Gene. It saddened her deeply. When they were together there was so much fire and passion, and to complicate matters even more, she caught herself thinking about Dale quite a bit lately.

Polly was twenty-one years old; old enough to go into bars. Sally, her dog, was also twenty-one years old and had been quite ill for some time. Her brother Sonny had no choice but to take Sally behind the barn and shoot her in order to put her out of her misery. It broke Polly's heart. She had loved Sally so much that she cried for days. Sally had been her best friend, and now she was gone. Polly recalled all the good times she and Sally had had when they were together. They had been together since Polly was just a little girl. Sally was smart and very protective of Polly. She even seemed to know when Polly would be home for the weekend because she would be waiting by the gate for her. Now Sally was dead and Polly felt so alone! She went behind the barn to the place where Sonny had buried Sally and knelt at her grave. Polly buried her head in her hands and cried until there seemed to be no more tears left. Of all the things that had gone wrong in Polly's life thus far, this was the worst. She walked away, glancing back at the little mound of dirt adorned by a little cross and a few flowers. It's been said that time heals all wounds. With each passing day, Polly began to miss Sally less and less.

Polly found herself falling in love with Dale. She had been determined not to marry until she was twenty-one years old. All of her friends were getting married, and she was beginning to wonder if she would ever get married. She was tired of sleeping alone, and she wanted some passion in her life.

At the bank, she was a "floating" teller and worked on diverse assignments for the management level staff. She would often find herself daydreaming about Dale. One Friday, Dale picked her up at work. They stopped at Bennett's Drug Store and shared a large cherry coke, after which they went to Polly's house so she could freshen up. Dale told her he would pick her up at 8:00 p.m.

When Dale picked her up, Polly asked him what plans he had for them that night. He told her his parents were out of town, and they had the whole house to themselves and could do whatever she felt like – dancing, watching TV, or listening to the radio. She told Dale that whatever he wanted to do was fine with her. He kissed her gently on the lips, and they cruised through town, as was the custom when on a date. When they were done cruising through all the local hot spots, they drove to Dale's house.

The house was a fairly new home furnished in Early American. The place was spotless. Dale offered Polly a beer, which she accepted. He opened one for himself as well. After a couple more beers, they were both feeling a bit tipsy. As they sat on the couch, they looked at each other with lust in their eyes. They reached for each other and began kissing with intense passion. Their breathing became heavy as Dale led Polly by the hand to his bedroom.

Dale's bedroom was not as clean as the rest of the house, but Polly didn't care. The only thing on her mind was romance. As they lay on the bed, he kissed her not too gently on the lips. Their kissing rose to a feverish crescendo of passion. They disrobed and the foreplay began. They slowly explored each other's bodies. Dale was crazy about Polly. Actually, he had always had a secret crush on her. They were totally uninhibited as they made love. The climax of their passion echoed throughout the house. That night, they made love several times, each time just as incredible as the first time. That night they fell in love!

They began seeing each other every day. Polly's parents didn't seem to approve of Dale either, but at this point in her life, she didn't care what they thought. She had decided to live her life the way she wanted to. She was well aware of Dale's heavy drinking, but she was caught in the web of his extraordinarily good looks and incredibly passionate lovemaking. She even entertained the thought of marrying him. Most of her friends were either married or getting married, and she was beginning to feel left out.

After a few months of serious dating, Polly asked quite bluntly, "Dale, what are your intentions? Do you plan on marrying me?" She also told him, "If marriage is not in your plans, I'm moving back to Minneapolis and marrying Gene." Dale's eyes grew wide. Polly had caught him completely off guard. He was totally speechless for a moment, then he responded, "Yes, I want to marry you, but it never occurred to me that you felt the same way." Polly told him, "Well, I do feel the same way. I don't want to be an over-the-hills bride. If we're going to get married, I want to do it while I'm still young." Dale then asked, "Well, when do you want to get married?" Polly told him she wanted to marry him as soon as possible. She said, "I'll tell my parents we're getting married and we'll begin making plans." This conversation occurred while they were on the dance floor of the Hollyse Hawk Ballroom in Hatfield, Minnesota.

They had both been drinking and were feeling quite romantic. When the dance was over, they made love in the back seat of Dale's car. It didn't matter where they made love, it was always incredible.

CHAPTER 17

Having made the decision to get married, Polly and Dale both began to feel a bit nervous. Polly had some regrets about breaking it off with Gene, but her parents had been against their relationship from the onset. She thought of him often, but knew it would never have worked out between them.

When Polly informed her parents that she and Dale were getting married, they protested. They were well aware of his carousing and heavy drinking. But even though they didn't approve, Polly was twenty-one years old and had the right to make her own decisions. Polly told her parents that she and Dale were going to be married as soon as possible.

Dale was working at a local hardware store and not making very good money. It was, however meager, an income. Polly was making better money at the bank. They could afford to live solely on her income. Polly decided to have a small wedding. She called her best friend, Lenore, in Minneapolis and asked if she would be her maid of honor. Lenore said she'd love to. Dale asked his older brother Wilbur to be his best man. As the wedding day got closer, they both got nervous. Polly daydreamed about what it would be like being married to Dale, and her face would flush. She was tired of sleeping alone. Now she could have sex whenever she wanted.

Ever since she was a little girl, Polly had been boy crazy. She had experienced many different crushes on so many different boys. She had an insatiable appetite for men. Now she would be marrying the man she had longed for.

On August 20, 1950, a private wedding was held at the Hofelman Ranch. Only a few selected friends, mainly neighbors, attended the ceremony. Polly wore a Swedish style dress that ended just a few inches above the knee, and a short veil that partially covered her face. She looked exquisitely beautiful. Dale was dressed in a dark blue suit that made him look devastatingly handsome. They were married by a Methodist Minister. Polly's parents cried when the vows were exchanged. Their tears were not tears of joy, they were tears of sadness and frustration. They knew the kind of man Dale was, but were helpless in preventing the union between Polly and Dale. Their baby was now a woman who had made her own choice.

No sooner was the wedding ceremony over than Dale began drinking. The guests offered their congratulations to the bride and groom as more tears were shed by her friends with whom she had grown up. The happy couple cut the wedding cake. As the cake and punch were being served, Polly couldn't remember a time when she had felt happier than she did at this moment. Every time she looked at Dale, she reminded herself how fortunate she was to be married to him, and she hoped everything would work out. When the celebration was over, the couple left on their honeymoon.

Dale and Polly drove to Mitchell, South Dakota. By the time they arrived, Dale was already fairly drunk. They rented a motel room. Polly was really excited about her wedding night. This was a moment she had long anticipated. To her utter dismay, the moment they entered the room, Dale passed out. Needless to say, Polly was extremely disappointed. This night had not turned out the way she had always dreamed it would.

Early the next morning, Dale made love to her, and once again she was happy. Now everything seemed perfect. Later that day, they drove to Black Hills. All they had was thirty dollars for their entire honeymoon. Dale got drunk every day. At this point, Polly had only one thought, 'If this is a taste of what lies ahead, this marriage is doomed to fail.' The honeymoon was one big disappointment for Polly.

When they returned from their honeymoon, they rented a small house. For the first few days, Polly was walking on air. Dale was attentive and loving. She felt totally content and happy. If they put a quarter in their piggy bank for every time they made love, they would be able to afford a house in no time. They were young and full of energy. Life was good!

Dale went to work at the hardware store and Polly worked at the bank. She loved her work. She never missed work, not even when she was sick. She believed in saving her money and that's exactly what she was going to do. She wanted to buy a house, and she knew the only way to accomplish that was to save, save, save.

Polly sometimes remembered the good times she had had in Minneapolis, but she was glad her father had talked her into coming home. She also thought about her wedding day and felt bad for having made her parents cry, which, in turn, had made her cry.

On the weekends, Polly and Dale would visit her parents. Her mother would prepare a large meal and they would stuff themselves. After they left her parents' house, they would visit Dale's mother. His father had died when Dale was in the Navy. Dale was discharged as a hardship case so he could go home and take care of the family. Instead of taking care of the family, he spent most of the time getting drunk with his friends. It was, in his opinion, the manly thing to do. It was "macho". No matter how sick he felt the following day, it didn't stop him from getting drunk again.

Polly began seeing a side of Dale she didn't much care for. Every day after work he would stop at the bar for a beer in order to unwind from a hectic day at work - or so he said. He had begun to drink quite heavily. There were times when he would get home late, which would upset Polly. He would say he was sorry, promising never to do it again. The following day it would happen all over again. After work, he'd stop at the bar and stay till closing time. Polly was getting really tired of his routine and his bullshit, so she decided to lay down the law. Either he stopped coming home late or she was moving out.

Dale knew she meant what she said, so he started going straight home after work. She told her parents about his drinking problem and asked for their help. The advice they gave her was to drink right along with him. That didn't work because he drank like a fish. He drank most of the money he earned. Polly was at her wit's end. She kept asking herself how she could have been crazy enough to have married Dale. Somewhere deep inside, she knew the answer – she loved the man. She was determined to work at saving her marriage.

One month, Polly missed her menstrual period. She knew what that meant. She became angry at herself for not taking the necessary precautions. As much as Polly wanted to have children, she felt that this was not the most opportune time to start a family. But since she was already pregnant, the decision was out of her hands. She had morning sickness every day for the first three months. Her body was going through the normal changes brought on by pregnancy, and she had begun to put on weight. She felt fat and awkward. As her pregnancy progressed, her belly grew to the point where she could no longer see her feet. The baby growing inside of her had begun to move a lot, and when she and Dale felt it kick they both got very excited. As her delivery date got closer and closer, they became nervous in anticipation.

The day finally arrived. Their son Larry was born. It was one of the most incredible days of their lives. The baby's grandparents were ecstatic. Dale was so awed by the birth of their son that for a long period of time he quit drinking. Polly gave birth to her son on Friday and was back to work on Monday. She was a truly remarkable woman with great inner strength and resiliency.

After the novelty of fatherhood wore off, Dale began drinking again. A couple of weeks after he had started drinking again, Dale drove to Sioux Falls, South Dakota. He got so drunk he hit seven parked cars and got thrown in jail. He was in a lot of trouble!

Dale called Polly to bail him out. Having decided that he could clean up his own mess, she refused his request. It might just teach him a lesson. Dale was a good man, but it was obvious that he needed the kind of help that Polly couldn't give him. He was, without a doubt, an alcoholic, and needed the professional help and counseling that only a rehab center could give him.

After he got out of jail, Polly suggested that he seek professional help. He agreed to do it for her. She told him to do it for himself, before he ended up killing himself or someone else. She also told him that he'd better get his act together because she was sick and tired of his drinking and total lack of ambition. Polly said to him, "You need to get a grip on your life. You need to set goals. You need to learn a trade because being a hardware man won't get you very far." After thinking about it for a while, he told Polly he had always wanted to be a barber. She offered to help put him through school if that's what he really wanted. She said, "I've saved enough money to help you pay for your schooling if you're really serious about learning the trade." The only barber school was in Minneapolis. Dale and Polly inquired about the school, and Dale decided to start in September.

Time was moving so quickly. Little Larry was already three months old. He was their little treasure. They both doted on their son.

Dale had to move to Minneapolis in order to attend barber school and get away from his drinking buddies. He returned home on weekends to be with his family. Unfortunately, his incessant drinking continued. He kept telling himself that he was going to quit, but his urge to drink was just too powerful. He knew he had to get help soon before his whole life went down the toilet. Dale was determined that even though he couldn't stop drinking, he would at least try to finish barber school.

The first few days in Minneapolis proved to be very lonely for Dale. He missed his son and his wife very much. He was still very much in love with Polly and hated being away from her. He longed for the day when they could be together all the time, just like a real family. Every time he became depressed he headed straight for the bar, where he and his school buddies would get loaded. The next day he would go to school feeling like he had been run over by a Mack truck.

Polly continued working at the bank while Grandma Lillian took care of little Larry. He was a very good boy who never got into any mischief. Lillian loved having him around. He occupied her empty days. At night, Polly taught bridge to various organizations in Pipestone. It helped her keep her mind off Dale's absence.

Polly was very conscientious and took her job seriously. After the first year at the bank, she received a five thousand dollar bonus from her boss. She loved the banking business. She held a high profile and prestigious position. She loved being around so much money. Polly decided to invest her bonus money on a down payment for a house. The bank lent her the rest.

The house she bought had five bedrooms, and was located directly across the street from where they were living. Polly was going to have another baby and they needed the extra space. Dale was proud of the fact that Polly had the knack of making things happen. He couldn't imagine what he would do without her.

After Dale had completed his 1200 hours of barber school, he opened his own barbershop in downtown Pipestone. He was doing much better at controlling his drinking. As a family they were getting along, and the arguing had subsided somewhat. Being apart for a year had done wonders for their relationship. It was apparently what they needed to get their marriage back on track.

Little Larry was growing like a weed. He was, however, very spoiled. Polly gave birth to her second child, a girl, and named her Patti. At first, little Larry was very jealous of her because he was no longer getting the attention he had become accustomed to, but it didn't take too long for him to come to accept his baby sister. He liked having someone to play with.

Dale's barbershop developed quite a reputation, and before long he had to hire two other barbers to help with all the customers he had acquired. Dale Laffrenzen had finally grown up and become a responsible father, husband, and businessman.

On weekends, they would invite friends over to play cards and have a few social drinks. Dale, however, had not learned what "social drinking" meant. He always managed to get drunk. Polly felt very dejected at the thought that Dale would probably never change.

CHAPTER 18

Ken missed Pipestone and decided to return from California. Even though he still loved Polly, he had met and married a girl named Verna. He still had a special place in his heart for Polly, but he loved Verna very much. Ken and Verna were amongst the friends who had been invited to play cards with Dale and Polly. Ken had been Polly's first real love. He was in the Army National Guard and had been placed on active duty. During the course of the evening Ken told Polly that he would be going to Korea, where there was a big war going on between North and South Korea, Communist forces against American forces. Seven years after WWII, America was entrenched in a ferocious battle with Communist insurgents. The enemy was ruthless, but Ken told Polly that he wasn't afraid to die. The news saddened her because after all, she had been in love with him, and in many ways she still loved him. He would always have a special place in her heart. They embraced, and she told him he'd better not get killed overseas because if he did, she would kill him when he got home. They looked at each other and laughed. A tear rolled down Polly's cheek as she told Ken she would miss him.

The following Monday, Ken's entire unit left for Alabama to prepare for their journey into the unknown battlefields of North Korea. The tragedy was that again, many Americans were losing their lives. When diplomacy no longer works, the only alternative seems to be war. This was supposedly a police action and not a full-blown war. War was never declared. While Ken was waiting for his unit to be sent to Korea, he became a Drill Sergeant. He was the kind of Drill Sergeant who would get in your face if you weren't doing your job right. Most of the new recruits didn't care for him much. Behind his back they referred to him with horribly profane names. But Ken didn't care what anyone thought of him. His job was to get these young recruits ready for combat even if it meant being unpopular.

When he first joined the Army National Guard nobody had been easy on him, and that fact served to make him a better soldier. Some of the young kids he was responsible for training were destined to go to North Korea and do battle with Communist insurgents, and it was his job to prepare them for the horrors that awaited them. Most of the men didn't like being in the Army, but as soldiers it was their job and responsibility to serve and protect their country. It wasn't an easy job, but someone had to do it. Ken was sharp, and set an excellent example for the men under his command.

After being a Drill Instructor for a year, his unit was separated and became a piecemeal unit. Ken boarded a ship in California that would take them to Korea. During their grueling journey, a lot of the men on the ship got seasick and puked continually. At times, Ken felt as if they would never arrive at their destination. It seemed a very long time since they had left Pipestone. Ken hated the idea of leaving his beloved wife Verna behind. He really missed her and longed for the day when he could see her again, hold her in his arms, and make love to her. He loved her so very much. He wrote her a letter every chance he got. At night he would walk out on the deck of the ship and look up at the stars, and wonder if he would survive his tour of duty in Korea. He felt so alone.

By the time the soldiers arrived in Korea, they were all sick of being on the ship. Korea had mountains that reminded him of the Black Hills back home. Two days after getting off the ship he was with a new unit out in the field. He got attached to a mortar company, and his new assignment was as a forward observer for the 81 Millimeter Mortar Platoon. He would spy on the enemy and then call in the grid coordinates. Being right in the enemy's lap, some-times he was scared shitless, especially when all the enemy's mortar rounds started saturating his area. The thud they made scared the hell out of him.

There were mountains as far as the eye could see, and it was starting to get chilly at night in the high-lands. The first few days in Korea were far different than anything he had ever experienced in his life. The culture and the people were peculiar. Many things about this country were different. It would take a lot of getting used to. Ken had never imagined he would be fighting a war at the age of twenty-one. Now he was all alone in the middle of it staring off into total darkness, wondering what the enemy was up to. Eat-ing cold C-rations was not something he liked doing. Sleeping in a cold bunker cut into the side of a moun-tain was downright uncomfortable, and the damp-ness from the condensation penetrated the clothing he was wearing, causing him to shiver as he tried to sleep.

In the morning, he went out on patrol seeking the enemy. That night, as he started to fall asleep, he heard a shrieking sound followed by a loud explosion that shook the earth around him. He prayed that a mortar wouldn't make a direct hit on their bunker. The barrage lasted several hours. Before the night was over his nerves were shot. He didn't get any sleep at all that night. All he could do was think of how wonderful it would feel to be in a soft warm bed with his wife beside him.

At the crack of dawn, he was heating himself a cup of coffee to ease the chill in his bones. The platoon leader briefed him on his assignment for the day. He checked his M-1, making sure it was ready in case he was confronted by the enemy. As he walked down the trail heading in a northerly direction, Ken was scared because he did not know what he would encounter. With a map in his hand, which was sweating profusely, and his private thoughts, he moved briskly along the narrow path that had been carved into the side of a huge eminence. As he walked, he was cautious, and panned his rifle from side to side looking for the enemy. His heart was beating so fast that he could actually hear it as it palpitated out of control. As he continued to move slowly, he could hear loud explosions and small arms fire everywhere. There was one hell of a war going on out there and men were dying. At times he wondered why they were fighting at all. All he knew was that he had a job to do and he would do it to the best of his ability, even if it meant losing his life on foreign soil.

Every little noise he heard startled him. He was now in the jungle, where the foliage was very thick. He had no idea where he was. If it weren't for his map and compass, he would already have gotten lost. He could hear American planes flying overhead on a bombing run. He could also hear loud explosions up the valley from where he was, and soon after that he could hear the planes returning to base camp to reload with more bombs. He was now getting close to the area where the Americans suspected the encampment of a hostile insurgent regiment was located.

As he continued to walk, he could hear voices not too far from his present position. The sound was foreign to his ears. He was sure it was the enemy, and his heart immediately began to race. It was so loud it made a thumping sound. As he moved in a northerly direction down the same path, everything suddenly seemed to get darker. He moved off the trail so the brush would camouflage him and he could shield himself from the enemy.

He needed to call in his present location. The voices he kept hearing were definitely foreign. As he spoke into the mike of his radio, he said, "Mac 1 Mac 1, this is Charlie Horse 1 over." (Voice on radio)" Yea, this is Mac 1 over." Ken said, "Yea Mac 1, I just wanted to give you my position. I am about 5 clicks north from your position over." "Charlie Horse 1 hear you loud and clear, out." As Ken sat on the ground, he took out his canteen and drank some water. He was sweating profusely, and the sweat kept running down the side of his cheek. He took off his helmet and wiped his face with his hanky. Sporadic gunfire and loud explosions were still going off all around him.

He could still hear those voices and knew he would have to investigate the situation, so without making any noise, he set out to see where the voices were coming from. He was hesitant, but he had to do it because it was his job. He took off down the same path he had been on. He came to a ravine, and as he peered through the thick foliage, he could see smoke billowing upwards. He could smell the aroma of rice being cooked by someone. As he got closer he could detect that they were Koreans talking, but he didn't know if they were friend or foe. He moved very cautiously closer to where the noise was coming from, and noticed about ten North Korean soldiers sitting around their little encampment eating rice out of a bowl and speaking really fast. It seemed as if none of them were paying attention to their duties. Ken sat watching them for a moment, and once he decided they were the enemy, he pulled out his map and checked the numbers. Once he had the grid and co-ordinates correct, he spoke into the mike and told his unit to send a Willie Peter for a marker round. He waited about three minutes, and then heard a shriek-ing round go over his head and explode close to where he was. Once he saw that it was on target, he called again and told them they were on target, and to go ahead and cut loose with everything they could mus-ter. In two minutes the mortars were hitting their target. He could see the soldiers getting hit. Some tried to run only to be hit by more rounds. He spoke into the mike again, then got up and made his way back to camp. He felt good about his accomplish-ment on his first assignment.

When he got back to camp, he gave himself a whore's bath. He was completely soaked with per-spiration, not from exertion but from nervousness. After bathing, he built a small fire so he could heat his C-rations. He was tired of eating cold food.

Ken had only been in Korea a few days and was already very homesick. He longed for a letter from his wife. He missed her with all his heart. Once ev-eryone was back in camp they would have mail call. The worst kind of mail was a "Dear John" letter. Many soldiers committed suicide as a result of these "Dear John" letters. The thought of another man sleeping with their girl just didn't sit well with them, and without the one they loved they had no reason to live. Dying was the easy way out.

That night Ken sat deep inside his bunker. Bunkers were built into the side of the mountain, and they were cold and damp. That night the enemy mortared the hell out of their camp all night. He didn't get any sleep at all. In the morning he was still tired when he went out on his mission. Spying on the enemy was an exciting job. When he was all alone deep in the jungle, he felt better than he did when he was inside the dark dungeon.

His tour of duty in Korea was far worse than he could ever have imagined. The explosions, carnage, and fear were beyond description.

Forty-eight days after arriving in Korea, Ken was hit by a mortar round. The red hot shrapnel hitting his body was so painful that he screamed. He had never felt such excruciating pain in his life. The thought of dying crossed his mind and he began to panic. The last thing he wanted to do was die in North Korea. By the time the medic got to him, he was half-conscious, and the only picture in his mind was that of his wife. He didn't want to die. He wanted to go home and grow old with her. He wanted children, especially a son. Now his life was hanging by a thin thread. He was med-evaced to a medical unit where he could get the medical attention he needed. Once they stopped the bleeding, he was out of danger. The shot of morphine they gave him made him feel much better. He became too relaxed to feel any panic.

A couple of days after being critically injured he had to be airlifted to Japan. During his recuperation, he got orders sending him to work on ships cleaning decks. It beat the hell out of being in the field sleeping in a cold musty bunker. Besides, he had more time to write letters to his wife. He also wrote to Polly about his many experiences and the fact that he had been critically wounded. After that, he began getting letters from a lot of his friends in Pipestone. It lifted his spirits to know that his friends still cared and that he hadn't been forgotten. Once his tour was over, he was going back to Pipestone. Even though Pipestone was a little hick town, it was in his blood, and there was no other place on earth like it. It would forever be a special part of his life. It held many fond memories for him.

CHAPTER 19

$\mathbf{D}$ale eventually began drinking heavily again, and his employees began to complain to Polly. This really infuriated her. She tried every conceivable way to embarrass him. She even went as far as going out on the street naked. Nothing worked. He was a chronic alcoholic who needed professional help. He was self-destructing and couldn't seem to stop. He even started losing those customers who were his best friends.

Polly finally came to the realization that she had made a big mistake in marrying Dale. He was sick, and there seemed to be nothing she could do to help him. They fought constantly because of his drinking. Polly, feeling helpless and totally disappointed with her husband was glad she had her parents to lean on. One night, her Grandfather Hofelman had been found frozen to death on the side of the road. He drank a lot and had apparently passed out, ultimately freezing to death. Polly had never been really close to her Grandfather Hofelman. Because of his drinking his own son, Art, had stayed away from him. He had been a mean and cantankerous drunk.

Polly could see that Dale was headed in the same direction, and she didn't want to be around to watch it happen. She gave him an ultimatum: either he stop drinking or she would file for divorce! She made him move out of the house, and wouldn't even talk to him. Dale would call Polly at the bank and beg her to take him back. He always promised he would quit drinking, but she told him she had heard that many times before. She could no longer put up with his drinking, and if necessary she was prepared to raise the children all by herself without his help. Polly was a very self-sufficient woman who was not afraid of work. Besides, these days he was a real pain in the ass.

Polly became more involved in community service in an effort to get her mind off her failing marriage. Her children were the most important concern in her life right now. If Dale wanted to drink himself into an early grave, then let him go right ahead. She wasn't going to stop him. His once very handsome face was beginning to show signs of deterioration as a result of his drinking. His body reeked of liquor. He hadn't shaved in days, and looked more like a hobo than a businessman.

After work, Polly would sometimes drive by Dale's barbershop and see that it was closed. Evidently he was spending more time at the bar than at the shop. He continued calling Polly almost every day, begging her to let him come home. He told her he desperately needed his family and that he would really try to quit drinking. He wore her down. Feeling sorry for him, she finally agreed to let him come home but told him he had to sleep on the couch.

For the first few days after he had moved back home, he behaved himself and didn't have liquor in the house. If he was drinking, he was doing it somewhere else. As much as she hoped for a miracle, she knew that Dale was too far gone, and it was futile to believe that he could or would ever change. She tried very hard to accept him for what he was, a chronic alcoholic, in an effort to keep her family together, but she was devastatingly unhappy. Her job and her children were the only stable part of her life.

When Ken returned home from Korea, all of his friends gave him a big "Welcome Home" party. The party was held at Dale and Polly's house. There was a lot of drinking and celebrating. The whole town was ecstatic that Ken had made it home alive. Polly more than anyone was glad to see him. There was a special bond between them that would last forever. Before he left for Korea, Ken had married Verna, who was a good friend of Polly's. Ken and Verna visited Dale and Polly quite frequently. Excessive drinking was a big part of these get-togethers. On weekends, they would get together for cookouts and play cards till the wee hours of the morning. Since Ken had returned from Korea, Dale and Polly's house was filled with fun and laughter, but the drinking was still a problem. Polly tried to ignore it for the sake of the children.

Polly and Ken 1947

Polly and Dale, August 20, 1950

Polly Hofelman
Laffrenzen
1980

Emily Ann
1957

Polly and Walt
1985

Polly and Matt
1995

CHAPTER 20

Patti was now ten years old. One morning, after Dale had been out drinking all night and woke up feeling sick, Patti noticed how bad he looked. She knew something was wrong. She had been daddy's little girl from the day she was born. She knelt beside Dale, sobbing and begging him to stop drinking. Patti held his hand as he looked up at her and said, "Yes. I will stop drinking for you, baby." She looked him in the eye and asked, "You'll stop drinking for me, daddy?" Dale answered, "Yes. I will, pumpkin." She smiled and hugged him, telling him it was the happiest day of her life.

When Polly got home later that evening, Patti just had to share her good news with her mother. She said quite naïvely, "You're not going to believe what daddy told me. He promised me he was going to stop drinking. Isn't that good news, mommy?" Polly replied, "Yes it is, Patti." In the back of her mind, Polly doubted very seriously that Dale was capable of keeping his promise to his daughter. She had heard all of those empty promises before.

Dale was hell bent on keeping his promise to his daughter. To Polly's surprise, Dale didn't touch a drop of alcohol. A few days went by and he still hadn't taken a drink, but he was going through hell. He knew only too well that if he didn't stop drinking he was going to kill himself or someone else when he got behind the wheel. He wished he could have been a social drinker instead of an alcoholic. His alcoholism had caused so many problems for him, and most especially for his family. He was remembering the binges that lasted for days, worrying his family, who didn't know whether he was dead or alive.

He remembered the time that he had wrapped his car around a tree and left it there. When he got home, he told Polly he was going to use their other car, to which she responded, "Like hell you are!" When she turned her back, he took their piggy bank, a big metal box containing coins they had been saving for years, which amounted to approximately one thousand dollars. When Polly went looking for him, she found the car he had left wrapped around the tree, and she couldn't conceive how he had gotten out alive. When she saw the wreckage, she was beside herself knowing that he was still out there behind the wheel of their other car and he was still drunk. She was terrified that he would kill someone. That same night, the Sioux Falls Police Department called Polly to inform her that Dale was in jail. They wanted to know if she was going to bail him out, and she said, "No! There's no way I'm going to get out of bed just to get him out of jail! He can rot there for all I care!" She meant it too! She needed to get the moneybox filled with coins that Dale had taken, but decided she was not going to make the trip and hung up. Besides, she had to go to work in the morning. After she'd hung up, Polly was livid at the thought of all the trouble and anxiety this man was causing her, not to mention all the money it was costing her to stay married to him. She was so angry she wanted to strangle him with her bare hands.

Now, however, Dale was on his best behavior. He would go straight home after work instead of going to the bar, as had been his custom. Now that Dale was sober, things were looking up again and Polly was happier than she had been in a very long time. She was expecting their third child. Dale was happy when Polly told him she was going to have another baby.

During that summer, they went fishing at Lake Benton almost every week. Polly recalled the times when she and her father would go ice fishing in the winter. She had many precious memories of the things she and her father had done when she was a child. Being at Lake Benton brought back all her cherished childhood memories of the good times she had had with her father.

Larry and Patti swam near the shore while the grownups did the fishing. The beach was very sandy and kept very clean. They would set up their tents and spend the weekend under the stars. Campfires glowed all around the lake. Families would be sitting around these campfires telling scary stories as the children sat with their eyes opened wide listening intently. The sounds made by the night creatures made these stories even more frightening.

When Tommie was born, everyone was thrilled to have a new baby in the house. Baby Tommie was very handsome like his father. His birth was timely. It filled a void that seemed to exist in his family's life. Polly was ecstatic at the birth of her precious little boy.

Later on, Polly and Dale had another baby. This time it was a girl. They named their baby girl Judie. Polly loved all of her children equally and showed no favoritism. She proved to be a loving mother and devoted wife.

Everything seemed to have finally fallen into place. Their family life was good and they were doing well financially. Dale was working and some of his former customers were returning. Polly was constantly planning ways to improve their lives. She was an ambitious, resourceful, and diligent employee. She wanted to get ahead in life. She wanted to be somebody without having to struggle all the time. She tried to save as much money as she could, and had money in several banks. Deep down inside, Polly knew that even though things were going well at the present moment, her marriage would probably eventually deteriorate, and she was preparing for that day by putting as much money away as she could. Dale was oblivious of Polly's savings accounts and the money she was depositing into them.

A rumor was making the rounds that the Severeid family wanted to sell the Calumet Hotel for a dollar to anyone who wanted to buy it. Polly heard about it, and at the first opportunity went to see the Severeids to ask if the rumor was true. The Severeids assured Polly that it was true the hotel was on sale for a dollar. They told her they were literally giving it away because they didn't want to be taxed on the sale of the property. Without hesitation, Polly said she wanted to buy it. Hearing the urgency in Polly's voice, Mrs. Severeid told her she could have the Calumet Hotel for one dollar. Polly gave Mrs. Severeid the money, whereupon Mr. Severeid signed the deed over to Polly. Polly walked out of the Severeid's house knowing she had gotten a fabulous deal.

The famous Calumet Hotel now belonged to Polly. To some of the locals it probably didn't mean much, but it meant a great deal to Polly. All of the rock that had been used to build the hotel had come from Grandfather Johnson's quarries. The Calumet was filled with history.

When Polly got home, she told Dale, "You're not going to believe what I just did." Dale looked at her and asked, "What did you go and buy now?" She retorted, "How did you know I bought something?". Dale told her, "It's written all over your face." She told Dale that she had just purchased the Calumet Hotel for one dollar. The children, who were in their room, heard the news and came out jumping in excitement. Dale said in astonishment, "You're kidding!" Polly told him she wasn't kidding, and reached into her purse, took out the deed, and handed it to him. He stared at it for a moment, then handed it back to Polly. The kids were still jumping around repeating, "We're rich! We're rich!" Dale looked at Polly and said, "You're the most amazing woman I've ever met. You're always making things happen. I don't know how you do it. I guess you have a very special gift." For the rest of the night Polly was walking on air.

The following day, the family went to go see the hotel. They explored all of the rooms and hidden corridors of the most infamous hotel in southwestern Minnesota. It now belonged to Polly. She had been given an opportunity that comes once in a lifetime. As they looked around, they could see it needed a lot of work. The former caretakers hadn't taken very good care of it. If Polly hadn't been with them, Dale and the kids would have walked out.

The Calumet needed a good cleaning, but this didn't faze Polly, who was used to hard work. To her it was just a minor obstacle. She was determined to resurrect the Calumet no matter how hard she had to work. She knew it was a dream come true.

Polly could hear voices from the past echoing in the hallways. Over the past hundred years, a multitude of people from different walks of life had at one time or another visited the Calumet Hotel. The people who had occupied the rooms had included businessmen, ordinary people, as well as ladies of the evening. There were people from different parts of the country who came to visit Pipestone's sacred quarries and purchase the famous red stone peace pipe. Many Indians in the surrounding area were still hard at work carving out the peace pipes that were sold in the stores around town. Some of the finest peace pipes were fashioned by the Indians in and around Pipestone. People traveled from all over the world to buy the famous red stone peace pipe. The Calumet Hotel had a great history, and Polly was going to do everything within her power to restore and preserve it.

There was talk that Urban Renewal wanted to knock down some of the old buildings around town. It infuriated quite a few people who lived in Pipestone. When Polly got wind of it, she was more determined than ever to preserve her hotel.

The first few days after they took over the hotel, Dale, Polly, and the children were busy cleaning the place up. It had been neglected for quite a long time. Even Polly's mother and father pitched in to help. They washed the sheets, blankets, and anything else that was washable.

Dale moved his barbershop into a space in the hotel that had once been a bank. The color scheme was magnificent! Polly was very proud of Dale for his effort, but she had the nagging suspicion that he was sneaking a drink now and then. He was, however, maintaining his sobriety.

They turned many of the rooms into apartments and office spaces. Ninety rooms were too difficult to maintain, so they closed the top floor, concentrating on the first two floors. They painted and wallpapered the rooms.

Polly quit her job at the bank because she had her hands full with the restoration of the most fabulous hotel in all of southwestern Minnesota. Polly was very proud to be the new owner. She was working her fingers to the bone trying to make this place as respectable as it had once been. Besides, an opportunity like this comes once in a lifetime, and she was determined to make the most of it.

In October, the furnace broke and would cost a lot of money to replace. She borrowed the money from the bank to replace it, but it would take several weeks before a new one could be brought in and installed. Meanwhile, the occupants of the hotel rooms were forced to wear layers of warm clothing. Some of the students who were staying at the hotel would huddle in the big room wrapped in blankets telling each other stories in an effort to forget how cold they were. The four-foot thick walls were constructed of rock, and the cold seemed to permeate the walls, dropping the temperature to freezing inside the hotel. Polly was delighted that the students stuck by her despite the unbearable cold.

It was a blessing when the furnace finally arrived, but the installation process was time-consuming and tedious. The installers labored day and night. It was now the first week in November and it was really cold. The tenants and students patiently awaited the day when the job would be finished and they would have heat. In the meantime, Polly continued in her efforts to bring the hotel up to par. When the furnace was finally turned on, there was a grand celebration. It took a few days for the hotel walls to warm up again. Even Dale's customers were relieved to have heat again. Now that everything was back to normal and business was thriving again, laughter filled the corridors.

Polly loved music, so there was always a radio playing in some part of the hotel. She was always smiling and kidding around with the help. Her children loved living in the hotel because there was always something to do and life was never boring. Polly and Dale weren't making a great deal of money, but they made a decent living.

Pipestone was experiencing a very cold and snowy winter. Cleaning the snow from all the sidewalks around the hotel was an exhausting chore. It seemed they were always shoveling snow. The whole town seemed to be buried in it. All over town people could be seen shoveling as the children trudged through the snow having the time of their lives. The blowing snowflakes that swirled upward added a gleaming effect to the gray skies that had dumped tons of snow on every inch of Minnesota. It was extremely cold, but the whole state looked like a winter wonderland.

Already accustomed to freezing Minnesota winters, the children bundled up and played in the snow. Given the frigid winters, it must have been the inexpensive land and the tranquil atmosphere of Pipestone that attracted those who traveled from other states to settle there. It also had the best fishing lakes in the country. Pipestone flourished as new homes and buildings continued to be constructed.

Polly and her family were doing quite well financially. They even bought a new boat and took the
children to the lake, where they tried their hand at
water skiing. Every time they spent a day at the lake,
they were loathe to return to Pipestone, so they decided to buy a cabin in order to spend their weekends at the lake during the summer months. Living
in the hotel was nice, but life at the lake was blissful
and far more enjoyable. Before long, the kids were
getting quite good at water skiing, while Polly and
Dale enjoyed fishing.

At night, when everything quieted down around
the lake, the smell of fried fish permeated the air as
people cooked their catch of the day. Laughter could
be heard from the various camps, and the bonfires
helped to warm the chilly air. After all the difficult
times they had been through, Dale and Polly once
again began making love. Everything seemed so right
between them these days, and despite it all, Polly
still loved him. Dale was still a fantastic lover.

It had been a few years since Dale had taken a
drink, and he had become dedicated to his work. He
loved his family and felt fortunate to still have them
despite his sordid past. He still craved an ice-cold
beer every now and then, but knew that drinking
would only serve to destroy his marriage, so he chose
to overcome the temptation.

As the children grew older, they were able to help
out more with chores around the hotel. At times they
would bitch and moan about having to work, but
they knew that Polly wouldn't put up with their grum-
bling. They all had to do their share of the work.
Larry was in college and Judie was still too young to
help with the work, so Tommie and Patti had to carry
the load. Tommie was six-feet-six inches tall and quite

mature for his age. He liked tending the reservation desk at the hotel.

The busiest time at the Calumet Hotel was during the Pageant. People from all over the country converged at the hotel looking for a room to rent. Tommie was a "people person" and enjoyed conversing with their varied guests. He was as charming as he was handsome. He always made their guests feel welcome.

Just like their mother, Polly's children were very popular in school. During the weekend, the halls of the Calumet were inundated with the sounds of laughter and blaring music from the kids' stereos. Even though Polly wasn't crazy about the music the kids liked to listen to these days, she remembered how her parents hadn't cared for the music she listened to when she was young.

CHAPTER 21

The Vietnam War was raging in Southeast Asia, and many Americans were losing their lives. There were many Americans who opposed the war in Vietnam. Polly's oldest son was one of them. He decided he would rather escape to Canada than serve in a war he didn't agree with. Most Americans were in the dark as to the purpose of the Vietnam War. The soldiers who served in the War did so because they felt it was their duty as Americans, but had no idea what they were fighting for. As the War escalated, protests broke out on college campuses all over America. Many of Pipestone's young men and some women became soldiers who fought in Vietnam. Sadly, it was inevitable that some of them would lose their lives.

Polly concentrated on remodeling the Calumet Hotel and had very little time for anything else. It was a painstakingly time-consuming project, and it would be a long time before it would be completed. She had to keep the top floor of the hotel closed because it would be far too expensive to try and remodel the entire hotel. She was doing the best she could with the money she had available for the remodel, and sunk every penny she could into it. The Calumet was being remodeled one room at a time.

When business was slow, friends would come over to play cards, joke around, and reminisce about all the idiotic things they had done when they were in school and how special they felt being members of the Thirteen Nifty Teens Club.

The Calumet had great historical value. Many important people had been guests there at one time or another. Some of Polly's relatives were angry with her because she had purchased the hotel – especially one of her uncles. Many of the townspeople were jealous of Polly's good fortune to have purchased the hotel for just a dollar.

After a few weeks of hard work and determination, the Calumet began to take shape. The office buildings and Dale's barbershop were the focal points of the Calumet. Polly was proud of the progress he was making. He was in AA and wasn't drinking at all anymore. Polly had suffered so much anguish in the past because of Dale's drinking that she found it very difficult to trust him. Unconsciously, she anticipated with dread the day he would start drinking again.

A couple of years had gone by, and the remodel of the Calumet showed great progress. There were seventeen apartments, a law office, H & R Block, a real estate office, and numerous other businesses. Dale and Polly were doing very well.

For Polly, the restoration of this grand hotel was a labor of love. It held memories of her beloved grandparents. She was crushed when her grandparents died. Granny had been like a surrogate mother to her throughout the years. She had always been very supportive of Polly's endeavors. However, she never undermined nor interfered with Polly's and Lillian's relationship as mother and daughter. Granny had always been protective of Polly and wouldn't tolerate anyone causing her harm of any sort. Polly had always been spoiled by her grandmother. When she died, it broke Polly's heart. It took her a long time to get over her grandmother's death.

Urban Renewal offered Polly $42,000 for the Calumet. She told them there was no way in hell she would ever let them have the hotel. She knew what they wanted to do with it. As long as she was the owner of the hotel, she would never allow it to be torn down. She decided to register it as a Historical Landmark. It was one of Pipestone's treasures because without it, Pipestone would have been just another mediocre town. If it hadn't been for the Indians, the town of Pipestone might never have been established. The "Song of Hiawatha" had brought C.H. Bennett to the area and instilled in him the dream of building a town in this part of Minnesota. Had it not been for Mr. Bennett's dream, the Calumet Hotel would never have been built.

Even as a child, Polly had always been captivated by the magical intrigue of the Calumet Hotel. She fought to have it put on the National Docket in Washington, D. C. She even had a state Representative and Senator help her place it on the National Register. In 1978 she obtained a grant for half a million dollars so she could finish remodeling the Calumet Hotel. It was one of the happiest days of her life, and she wanted to share her good news with Dale. She anxiously waited for him to come home, but when she ran to him with her exciting news she discovered he was drunk. She was devastated. Even though, somewhere in the back of her mind, she had known this would probably happen, why did the son-of-a-bitch have to pick this most auspicious day to blow it? As far as Polly was concerned, this was the last straw. She couldn't and wouldn't put up with his drinking anymore.

Judie was twelve years old and staying with her older brother when Polly called to tell her that her father had started drinking again and she was leaving him. Tommie was a senior in high school, and Larry and Patti were married and no longer living at home. Polly had suffered the humiliation and anguish of living with an active alcoholic long enough. She had paid her dues and it was time to bail out. Despite the setbacks caused by Dale's drunken binges, Polly still had a strong spirit and lots of ambition. She had a fire inside of her, and she refused to let Dale's degrading behavior put it out.

Polly didn't know what the future held in store for her but she knew she had had enough. Dale couldn't have picked a worst time to resume his drinking. That night as she lay in bed, she was angry and just a little bit scared. She cried herself to sleep, cursing Dale for her misery. The following day, Polly packed her things and she and Judie left Pipestone. She had no idea where she was going. She drove towards South Dakota. She drove till she began to feel tired. Judie was asleep. Polly kept thinking how well everything had been going and how Dale had managed to ruin everything. She knew she couldn't live like that anymore. She decided she was going to divorce Dale. Polly had worked so very hard to make her marriage work, forgiving Dale time and again and cleaning up his messes. This was one of the most despairing moments in Polly's life.

She had saved a little money, but it wouldn't last very long. She would have to find a job, and she had no idea what direction her life would take now. During the period that Dale had been sober she had looked to him for support and encouragement, and deep down she still loved him. In her mind, she looked for someone or something to blame for Dale's alcoholism – the town, his friends, etc. The only things Polly had ever wanted were to be loved and to be happy.

Polly had been driving the entire night and was in much need of sleep. In the distance she could see the lights of a city. She drove into the small town of Aberdeen. It looked like a nice little town. She drove down Main Street looking for a motel where she could rent a room. She could scarcely keep her eyes open. She was physically and mentally exhausted. She didn't know what the future held in store, but she did know that she and her children were sick and tired of Dale's drinking. It had caused a lot of havoc in their lives. She loved Dale but could no longer put up with him, and if she had to live out of a suitcase, then so be it.

Polly rented a small but clean room. When Judie got out of the car she was half-asleep. She stumbled slowly into the room, and the first thing she did was turn on the TV Polly carried in the suitcases and decided to take a nice long bath. As she soaked in the tub, she thought about the mess her life was in right now. She hadn't a clue how things could be so good one minute and go so wrong the next. The answer eluded her. The only thing she was sure of was that there was no way she would go back to Pipestone and live a life made miserable by her husband's drinking. She had been married to Dale for twenty-five years. There had been many memorable years, years when Dale had been sober. One of her fondest memories was when they bought the cabin on the lake. She remembered all the good times they had had at the lake with the children. As she lay in the tub, tears began to stream down her face. She felt so alone and scared! She would just have to take one day at a time. All the hard work she had put into remodeling the Calumet was all for nothing. The more she thought about it, the sicker she felt. When her head hit the pillow that night, she was so physically and mentally exhausted she fell instantly asleep.

In the morning, she and Judie had breakfast at a local cafe. They drove around Aberdeen checking out the sights. She liked this little town. She bought a newspaper and looked for a mobile home they might be able to afford with the little bit of money she had put away for a rainy day. She called several different homeowners before she decided on a small, two-bedroom mobile home that seemed to be in very good condition and was located in a suitable mobile home park. It was an older park that had been established in the mid-1960s. It was nicely landscaped with trees, bushes, and flower gardens, and it had sidewalks. The moment they saw the place, Polly and Judie fell in love with it. Judie liked the idea of having her own room. Polly was still distraught over her decision to file for divorce.

Polly decided to look for a job. She wore the best dress she possessed and carefully applied her makeup in an effort to make a good impression. Her first application was to the First National Bank. She had plenty of banking experience. She was hired immediately as a teller, which was right up her alley. She also applied at the Sheridan Hotel and got a job as a night auditor, as well as a part-time job at the Ramada Inn. With three jobs occupying her time she had very little time to think.

She enrolled Judie in school. A chip off the old block, Judie made friends quite easily. Judie's friends started hanging around the mobile home. They lived in a family-oriented mobile home park, and there were always kids around. The store wasn't very far away. Polly felt comfortable about leaving Judie alone while she worked. Judie was almost thirteen years old. Polly found it difficult being separated from her other children, but she was so busy working that she had little time to think about it. Although she had a very hectic and time-consuming work schedule, she didn't mind because she found the work fulfilling. The fact that she worked long hours kept her from dwelling on her precarious situation.

There were times, however, when Polly felt very much alone. Polly was the type of woman who could not live without a man. She had met a few men at work, but none of them interested her.

A few weeks after arriving in Aberdeen, she befriended the manager of the Super 8 Motel where she had spent the first night. She asked Polly if she would like to work for the Super 8 Motel. The manager told Polly that there were plans to build more Super 8 Motels. Polly thought about it for a while and said she would like to give it a try. No sooner had she put in her application at the Super 8 Motel offices than she was offered the manager's job in Pierre, South Dakota. She asked them where the hell Pierre, South Dakota was. The owner of the Super 8 Motel told her not to worry, it was just up the road. On May 21, 1978, Polly moved to Pierre, South Dakota as manager of the new Super 8 Motel.

Polly was lonely and missed Dale very much. She desperately needed male companionship. Dale missed her too, and decided to visit her. After twenty-five years, it was hard to let go. Despite the ugliness of their present situation they had shared many beautiful memories. In a moment of weakness, Polly agreed to give Dale another chance. The sexual part of their marriage had always been good, and it felt wonderful to be in his arms once more.

Dale promised for the umpteenth time that he would stop drinking. Polly and Dale smoothed things over, and Dale even got a job at a barbershop in Pierre, South Dakota. He cut back on his drinking for a while, but it didn't last. He went on a three-day binge and got so drunk that he blacked out. In his drunken condition he became abusive with Judie and Polly. His drinking progressed, and he spent a lot of time at the bars. Polly had a sinking feeling in her stomach that she should never have let Dale know where she was. Things kept getting worse. After a weekend of drinking, Dale would say he was sorry and promise never to do it again, but the following weekend he'd get drunk.

When Polly had finally had enough, she told him to get out of her house. Dale went ballistic and tried to choke her. He had her by the throat while Judie watched and screamed, "Please, daddy, don't kill my mother!" Polly was turning purple and her eyes had begun to bulge. She managed to blurt out, "Go ahead, kill me. You'll be doing me a favor by putting me out of my misery, you son-of-a-bitch." Dale loosened his grip a little and Polly screamed, "Kill me!" Meanwhile, Judie called the police, telling them that her father had gone off the deep end and was trying to kill her mother. Dale let go of Polly, and she started screaming furiously, "Get out of my house!" The police arrived and took Dale to jail.

Dale knew he had really blown it this time. There was no way Polly would ever forgive him. Polly, too, had learned her lesson. She could never trust this man again. He was now suffering from blackouts that scared the hell out of her. Ever since she had allowed him back into her life, Polly had become a nervous wreck. She was devastated by the fact that the man whom she had loved so passionately and lived with for so many years had actually tried to kill her. She had no doubt in her mind now that divorce was the only answer.

The following day, Dale called Polly from jail and asked if she would get him out. She adamantly refused, and told him that the only way she would drop the charges against him was if he left South Dakota. She was trembling as she hung up the phone. She couldn't believe the unmitigated gall of this man, expecting her to get him out of jail after trying to kill her. Dale agreed to Polly's terms and left South Dakota.

Polly was so distraught that she called her parents, tearfully relating the entire incident. She was so traumatized by the incident that she started losing her hair, and since she couldn't eat she began losing weight. The day she filed for divorce she had to be helped up the stairs of the courthouse building. All she wanted now was for this nightmare to be over. She wanted control of her life again. In her request for divorce the only thing she asked for was her freedom. He could keep everything else. Dale was given everything, including the Calumet Hotel and their cabin on the lake.

The day the divorce became final, it was as if a weight had been lifted from Polly's chest. She celebrated by going out on the town. She went to a bar where she met a lot of nice people playing pool and having a good time. Someone asked her if she would like to join them in a game of pool. She said she didn't know how to play the game but was willing to give it a try. Playing pool became her favorite pastime. She started going to the bar every night to play pool and hang out with her friends. It helped her forget her problems. It was good therapy because she was still going through hell. She knew it would take time to heal, and in the meantime, she put on a good front. Polly decided that what she needed right now was to start having fun. She even went dancing. None of this, however, interfered with her commitment to her position as manager of the Super 8 Motel.

CHAPTER 22

In November of 1978 her father passed away. Polly went back to Pipestone for the funeral. With everything that was going on in her life, the last thing she needed was having to attend her father's funeral. After the funeral, she returned to South Dakota and buried herself in her work. Her bosses really liked her because she was a hard worker and dedicated employee.

Polly was still young and full of life. In May of 1979 Tommie graduated from high school, and Polly and Judie drove to Pipestone for his graduation. Even if she couldn't stand the sight of Dale, she had to play it cool for Tommie's sake. She had to pretend that everything was all right. Polly had a knack for hiding her feelings. She could be cool on the outside even when she was seething on the inside.

She continued working hard at her job with the motel. She worked during the day but at night she liked going out and meeting new people. She was looking for a man because it had been quite a while since she had been intimately involved with one, and she was feeling lonely.

One night she had consumed quite a few beers. She longed for male companionship and intimacy. She met a man at the bar, and after closing time took him home with her. He made passionate love to her and she screamed in ecstasy. It had been a long time since a man had made love to her. After their passion subsided, she felt spent and completely satisfied. It had nothing to do with love – only sex. Polly had always been a very sensual and sexual person, and right now she wasn't looking for love, only sexual gratification. She had tried love, and it had only brought her grief and heartache.

At the Super 8 Motel she befriended a young woman named Peggy. Peggy came from a poor family. She and Peggy hit it off right away. As they shared life stories, they became the best of friends. They went night-clubbing together and played pool with the guys who hung around the pool tables. They had no qualms about sleeping with the men they met. These men weren't looking for long-term relationships or commitments. They were only looking for a "good time". Polly had always been sexually drawn to men, and now she and Peggy were fulfilling their desires without any permanent commitments.

Polly and Peggy hung around the bars and picked up a diverse selection of men who were also out for nothing more than a "good time". The girls were more than willing to accommodate them, and they both attracted their share of interested men. Peggy was a terrific listener, which is what most of the men were actually looking for.

During one of their nightly escapades, Polly met a very handsome man who in Polly's opinion seemed to have a lot of class. He had a formal education and was very articulate. Polly was interested in him and wanted to get to know him better. She was intrigued by his way of speaking and his sparkling eyes. Jack was in his early fifties, soft-spoken and in very good shape. Polly quickly became infatuated. Jack asked her to dance, and when he took her hand to lead her to the dance floor she was instantly aroused by his touch. As they danced, he held her close and kissed her in a way she had never been kissed before. He aroused her sexually. She wondered if she'd ever see him again. She had given him her home phone number and told him where she worked. She confided to Peggy her strong attraction to this stranger as well as her doubts that he would ever call her again. Peggy tried to reassure her that he would call just like he said he would.

Polly waited in somewhat doubtful anticipation for Jack's call. Finally one late afternoon, the man of Polly's dreams did call. By the time the long-awaited call came, Polly was totally unnerved. He invited her to dinner, and she nervously accepted.

Her date was at eight o'clock at night. It took Polly two hours to get ready. She looked ravishing! She wore one of her most beautiful gowns, which accentuated her long, attractive legs. Polly was now in her mid-forties but looked as good, if not better, than she did in her twenties. She had always taken good care of herself despite her many hardships. When her date saw her, he stared in utter awe at her beauty.

Judie, Polly's daughter, now lived with her sister Patti in Pipestone, and Polly lived by herself in the mobile home they had bought in South Dakota. Jack took Polly out to an elegant dinner at the Ramada. They engaged in idle chatter at dinner, which consisted of steak, lobster, and a very expensive wine.

After dinner they walked to a nearby nightclub. Polly had been married for twenty-five years, and it had been a long time since she felt as desirable as she did this night. As they danced, Jack held her sensually close, which made Polly feel attractive in a way she hadn't felt for a very long time.

Polly was having such a good time and feeling so good about herself as a woman that time seemed to stand still. Polly had always been acutely aware of her sexuality. Now as Jack held her close, that part of her being was unleashed and she could no longer contain herself. It was no wonder that this night had turned into a night of tumultuous passion. The expertise with which Jack made love to her satisfied her most intimate desires. Never had she felt such sexual fulfillment. As she slept, her erotic dreams made her feel sated and sexually fulfilled.

Jack and Polly began dating each other exclusively. Within time, he told Polly that he was married and had three children. Polly didn't care, and in no uncertain terms told him so. She reveled in the way he made her feel, and to Polly that was all that mattered. She told him that married or not, she just wanted to be with him. Since Polly didn't expect more from him than he could give, and since he was totally crazy about her, they continued seeing each other.

One Sunday afternoon, Jack called Polly and invited her for a ride in his private airplane. Polly had never been on a plane before and was quite apprehensive. Jack told her there was nothing to worry about as he had extensive flying experience. At first Polly was reluctant, but after some thought, she became excited about experiencing something new.

Jack filed his flight plan, and he and Polly headed towards Pipestone. After her fears had subsided she began to enjoy the airplane ride. From the plane, everything looked astoundingly beautiful and minute. The farmlands resembled a great big jigsaw puzzle. Polly was having a great time!

The skill with which Jack maneuvered the airplane totally amazed her. He was so enigmatic and yet so self-assured that she became completely enthralled with this man. As he reached out and squeezed her hand she knew she could very easily fall in love with him. She sensed the feeling was mutual as he looked at her and smiled. Polly had always been a very intelligent woman, and she could converse with Jack in a way she had never been able to do with any other man.

In the distance Polly could see Pipestone. It looked so small from up in the air. When they landed, Polly's mother was waiting for them. They drove to the ranch, where Lillian had prepared a delicious meal. Lillian was getting on in years and had been alone since her beloved Art had passed away. Polly missed her father so much that the thought of him being gone made her cry. She had always been daddy's girl. Her brother Sonny was married and had a family of his own.

Visiting Pipestone stirred up a lot of great memories for Polly. She really missed her grandmother. Finally it was time to leave, and Polly and Jack bid farewell to Lillian and Pipestone. It had been a great day!

After they returned to Pierre, South Dakota, Polly and Jack went to Polly's place, where they spent hours making love. Jack had fallen so deeply in love with Polly that he asked her to marry him. She had to remind him that he was already married. He told her he would divorce his wife so he could be with her. Jack was such an intelligent, capable man and such a marvelous lover that the idea greatly appealed to Polly. Jack and Polly became almost inseparable. When they weren't speaking to each other by phone they were doing something together. Polly loved flying in Jack's airplane, and they flew to a variety of exciting places.

Finally, Jack asked his wife of many years for a divorce. She told him she would never divorce him. As far as she was concerned it was "Till death do us part". She knew Jack had been cheating on her. They rarely made love any more, and he always made excuses when he was away from home for long periods of time. His betrayal wounded her deeply, but there was no way she was ever going to give him up.

Polly and Jack continued seeing each other as often as they could. One Saturday morning, Jack asked Polly if she would like to fly to Wisconsin with him to visit some friends. He told Polly he wanted to take his two children as well. Polly refused to accompany him. She knew he was married, but she didn't want to subject his children to an encounter with "the other woman". He pleaded with her to go, but she adamantly refused. He told her he wanted her to get to know his children and vice versa. She knew he meant well, and she really did want to go, but she didn't feel right about it. That afternoon, as they stood in the doorway of her apartment, she said goodbye to Jack and watched as he walked away. Polly had never liked saying goodbye, and for some inexplicable reason she had a sinking feeling in her stomach as she saw Jack walking away.

The following morning she received a phone call at work from a friend who asked if she had heard what had happened to Jack. She said, "No." Her friend told her that Jack had been killed in an airplane crash somewhere over Iowa. Polly couldn't believe what she was hearing. She asked her friend to repeat what he had said. Her friend said, "Jack was killed in a plane crash yesterday." She dropped the phone and screamed, "Oh, my God! No, please, not Jack! Jack can't be dead!" She began to cry hysterically. Peggy rushed over to ask what was wrong. Polly couldn't stop crying. She told Peggy through her tears that Jack had been killed in an airplane crash. Then Peggy started crying. Polly felt as if her heart had been ripped out.

Polly looked up and saw Walt, a gentlemen she had met the day before when he checked into the hotel. Polly told Walt, an airline pilot, that Jack had been killed in an airplane crash. She then asked Peggy to take over the front desk because she needed to be alone. Peggy told Polly not to worry. She would take care of business, and Polly could take as much time as she needed.

Polly walked into her bedroom and took out a picture of Jack. The tears came flooding out again. She couldn't stop crying. She felt as if a part of her had died. Jack was everything she had ever wanted in a man, and she had begun dreaming of spending the rest of her life with him. With his death, her dreams died too. She lay on her bed clutching his picture. In her dream state she felt Jack lying next to her. She could actually feel the comfort of his arms around her and hear his gentle voice telling her how much he loved her. He told her that their love for each other was timeless, and even though he could not be with her physically, he would forever be in her heart, and by virtue of that love, she had to find the courage to go on. She awoke in a cold sweat. The unmistakable scent of her beloved filled the room. The pain in her heart was so intense, she began crying again. Knowing she would never see him again, feel his gentle touch or hear his sweet voice was too much to bear. Totally exhausted, she fell asleep.

In the morning, Polly got up, took a long bath, and returned to work. Even though she didn't feel like working, she knew it would serve to keep her mind off her misery. About ten o'clock that morning, Walt, the airline pilot, walked up to her and asked how she was feeling. He told her how sorry he was, and that he would be around for a few days in case she wanted to talk. Polly thanked him for his concern.

CHAPTER 23

Walt asked Polly out to dinner. Polly decided she needed someone to talk to, and accepted the invitation. They went to Tippers, one of the nicest restaurants in Pierre. Polly did all the talking while Walt just listened. He knew she was in a lot of pain. After a few hours of unburdening herself, Polly felt much better. After dinner Walt drove her back to her apartment and gave her a comforting hug before she went in. When she walked into her empty apartment, she began feeling depressed again. She hated being alone – especially now. The loneliness she felt was very oppressive. Her children were all grown up and no longer lived with her. She knew she had made many mistakes in her lifetime, and maybe this was her punishment. She filled the tub with warm water and soaked in it for a while. Relaxing in a warm bath always seemed to soothe her. Polly had known Jack for only a short period of time, but they had managed to fall in love. After a few days the pain of her loss began to subside a little. She had had a difficult life, and work had always been very therapeutic for her. She immersed herself in her work, just as she had always done when faced with difficulties and emotional pain. In the meantime, she and Walt had become good friends. He had grown really fond of Polly but didn't want to rush her. He knew she was going through a very difficult time, so he was content being someone she could talk to. Walt would be gone for days at a time, but upon his return he always rented the same room. Just like Jack, he loved flying. Soaring through the skies high above the clouds gave him an incredible peace. It was a real rush for him.

By choice, Walt was still single. He was never in one place long enough to form a lifetime commitment. Polly, however, seemed to be changing his way of life. When he was away from her, he could scarcely wait to see her again, and when he did see her again, his heart skipped a beat. He was totally attracted to her. Polly had been feeling very vulnerable since Jack's death, so when Walt asked her out she accepted. Polly was not the type of person who liked being alone, and even though she was still grieving for Jack she was in much need of companionship.

Walt and Polly dined at the finest places in Pierre. He was a perfect gentleman with Polly and never went any further than holding her hand. After dinner they would go dancing at one of the nightclubs in Pierre and have a few drinks. With each date they got better acquainted and began to discover each other's likes and dislikes.

Polly learned that Walt was an airline pilot for Southwest Commuter Airlines, which had flights coming in and going out of Pierre, South Dakota. He loved flying and even owned his own small private plane. He invited Polly to go flying on Sunday. She agreed because having flown with Jack, she had grown to love flying too. Polly anxiously looked forward to Sunday, when she got out of bed early, took her bath, meticulously applied her make up, and chose a nice casual outfit to wear. She had begun to care for Walt and wanted to look good for him.

Walt picked her up and they headed towards the airport. They boarded the plane, just as she and Jack had done so many times before. When they were airborne and soaring high above the clouds they both felt an incredible peace. The Black Hills always looked magnificent from the air, and the scattered farmlands resembled a patchwork quilt.

One of Walt's most important assignments was flying the Governor of South Dakota to different places around the State. On one occasion when Walt was scheduled to fly the Governor to a meeting, he invited Polly to accompany them. From then on Walt took Polly on most of his important assignments. It made Polly feel special. The pain of losing Jack had subsided. If Walt hadn't providentially come into her life when he did, Polly didn't think she could have recuperated as quickly as she had. She and Walt had become very good friends. Walt made Polly feel alive again!

Polly was scheduled to meet with key personnel of the District Office of the Super 8 Motel, which was based in Aberdeen, South Dakota. During the meeting, they informed her that they wanted her to go to Farmington, New Mexico to open a new Super 8 Motel that was being built there. She asked, "Where is Farmington, New Mexico?" They told her not to worry where it was because if she was willing, they would take care of all the arrangements so she could be there for the Grand Opening. She asked them if they were sure she was the one they really wanted for the job. They said that given her dedication, expertise, and loyalty, they had no doubt that she was the best qualified for the job. She was also informed that she would be receiving a sizeable raise. She asked them how soon they wanted her to leave and they said "Immediately!" Polly told them she would give it a try, and asked who was going to take over her present position in her absence. They told her they had chosen Peggy to take over.

The following day, Polly was on board a company jet headed for Farmington, New Mexico. It was the first time in her life she had been away from the Plains states. Along the way she became quite homesick. She wondered what New Mexico would be like. She had never been there and wondered if the people even spoke English. She was clueless as to what awaited her. After stopping in Denver to refuel, the plane flew across the Colorado Rockies. The view was breathtaking. She had never seen so many mountains in her life. As the plane carried her to her destination, Polly found it hard to believe that she had been entrusted with the opening of the new Super 8 Motel.

Farmington was nestled in a valley along the San Juan Mountains. All she could see was farmland and desert. It was totally different from anything she had ever seen. A company car was waiting to pick her up as soon as she landed. The driver was a handsome young man in his early twenties. He had a very nice smile and spoke with an accent. He chewed tobacco and sported a cowboy hat. She was reminded of the vacation she had taken with her parents to Texas. The memory brought a smile to her face. They finally arrived at the motel. She saw that it was much bigger than she had imagined.

Farmington was a typical American town. She noticed that it was populated by many Hispanics and

Native Americans, but the hustle and bustle was the same as any other town. Originally a small town, Farmington had grown with the introduction of new building developments. Progress had brought with it many new jobs for the people who lived in this community.

Polly observed the many new developments and welcomed the challenge that lay ahead of her. The motel was still under construction. It would be approximately six months before completion. It was Polly's responsibility to make sure the job was completed on time and to hire whatever help she needed to furnish each room as it was finished. She was a perfectionist and thrived on hard work.

Polly had been appointed the representative in charge of overseeing the building of the new Super 8 Motel. The supervisor of the construction company that had been hired to build the motel was a thorn in Polly's side. He was constantly undermining her authority. Polly refused to be intimidated by him, and never backed down in the face of confrontation. As far as she was concerned, this guy was a real jerk, and if she had been a man, she would have kicked his ass.

Living in Farmington was a radically different experience. There were several bars along Main Street. As in any other town in America, the young people cruised up and down Main Street. They drank and made a ruckus as they drove around. Polly knew it would take her a while to get used to this town, but she had already begun to make friends.

Walt called her to see how things were going, and said he wanted her home A.S.A.P. She told him it would be a long while before she'd be coming home. The motel was only half-finished and she was constantly locking horns with the contractor, a pompous son-of-a-bitch know-it-all.

Polly never knew what each new day would bring. She interviewed potential employees, which was no easy task. She tried really hard to get used to living in Farmington but found it quite frustrating. There were just too many things working against her. For the first time since she had arrived she was homesick. She missed Walt but she wasn't about to let him know it.

The closer the motel got to being completed, the more relaxed Polly became. She decorated each room with meticulous attention to detail. None of the rooms was identical. Each was decorated differently. One valuable lesson she had learned from her experience at the Calumet Hotel was that a guest's first impression as he walked into the room was of the utmost importance.

Polly hired a cleaning crew and made sure that each room was spotlessly clean. Along with cleaning and maintenance personnel, she also hired office and front desk help whom she personally trained. It took a lot of work and time before the motel was ready for its Grand Opening. The endless hours of work were exhausting. It would be a few more weeks before the Super 8 Motel would open. Polly could hardly wait to get back home. Walt was also anxious for Polly to return. Polly used every chance she got to daydream about Walt. He called her every night, and they would spend hours on the phone. Their relationship had begun to take on a new dimension. He told her how much he missed her and wanted her to hurry up and get home. She told him she'd be home before he knew it, that she wanted to wrap up the job as quickly as possible. Her assignment had been a great experience except for her encounter with the pompous and asinine construction boss.

It took Polly six months to train the personnel. Teaching people how to run a motel proved to be a difficult job because she had to deal with diverse personalities and mentalities.

The day finally arrived! The job was finished, and Polly happily flew back to Pierre, South Dakota. As the jet came in for a landing, she could hardly contain the joy and relief she felt at seeing her home again. But she knew she would probably be getting a new assignment, and wondered how long it would be before she would have to leave again. She also wondered what her new assignment would be and where it would take her. Part of her was a homebody, but another part of her welcomed new adventures. She had lived a sheltered life, and she was hungry to experience all that life had to offer.

She was relieved to be back home in her little apartment. She and Peggy talked for hours about her experiences in Farmington. She told Peggy she never wanted to go back there unless her job required it. Walt was ecstatic at seeing her again. For the first few days after her homecoming he didn't leave her side. Polly was flattered by his attentions.

On one occasion, Walt gave Polly a bouquet of flowers and asked her to marry him. She told him she thought he was a wonderful man but she wasn't ready for marriage just yet. Her marriage to Dale had been a traumatic disaster, and she was leery of making that kind of commitment again. She told Walt that he was everything she could hope for in a man. He was charming, handsome, intelligent, attentive, and a wonderful lover, but she just wasn't ready for marriage, and if he could handle it, she wanted their relationship to continue just as it was. Walt accepted her conditions. He wined her, dined her, and even took her flying just like before.

Polly had a feeling that her bosses were getting ready to send her on another assignment to open a new Super 8 Motel. Only they and God knew where her next assignment was going to be. Sure enough, just when she was beginning to really enjoy herself, she was summoned to the central office of the Super 8 Motel. During the meeting Polly was asked if she would like to go to Las Cruces, New Mexico to open a new Super 8 Motel, which was almost completed. She asked, "Where the hell is Las Cruces, New Mexico?" Again, they told her not to worry. They would take care of everything including the expenses involved in relocating. With some hesitation, she gave in. She told them she hoped it wouldn't prove to be as sour an experience as Farmington had been. They told her that the contractors in Las Cruces were very easy to get along with, so she had nothing to worry about. She asked if Peggy could go with her this time. They agreed to let Peggy accompany Polly, but said that Peggy would have to pay her own moving expenses.

Polly didn't know how to tell Walt that she had been given a new assignment and would be leaving Pierre again. She didn't want to hurt him because he had been so good to her since Jack's death. Ultimately, she decided to move to Las Cruces without telling Walt.

When the time came to start packing, Polly and Peggy squeezed Peggy's belongings through the window of Polly's bedroom so the movers would think that they were packing only Polly's belongings. It took the movers two days to load all of Polly and Peggy's belongings. The girls' cars were packed with their clothing and personal stuff.

CHAPTER 24

Polly and Peggy began their trip to Las Cruces, New Mexico. Polly had flown when she'd gone to Farmington, New Mexico, but this time their trip would be made by car. Neither girl had any idea how long it would take them to get to Las Cruces. They got on the road that would take them to New Mexico, not realizing what desolate terrain they were going to encounter. All they saw were farms here and there along with some small lakes. As they drove along Interstate 80 crossing Nebraska, all the farmhouses looked alike. Polly kept thinking, 'What have I gotten myself into?'

The girls stopped at rest stops along the way to stretch their legs, use the bathroom, and get something cold to drink. It was a long, boring, exhausting trip. The only thing that broke the monotony were the mountains in Colorado. They were breathtaking. Polly loved the mountains. She recalled the time she first visited Colorado. It was when her eldest son Larry was going to school at Colorado State University in Fort Collins. It had been her first encounter with the

Colorado Rockies. Their magnificence had taken her breath away.

By the time Polly and Peggy reached the New Mexico border, they were beyond exhaustion, and they still had to drive across the entire state of New Mexico. Polly kept thinking, 'We're never going to get there.' The rest stops were the only thing that revived them. They were unbearably miserable as they drove through the hot barren deserts of New Mexico.

When they finally arrived in Las Cruces, every inch of their bodies ached. Neither woman ever wanted to drive anywhere again as long as she lived. They were thrilled to see the Super 8 Motel, where they "crashed" for two days. When they finally awoke they were starving, so they went to a local café to get a bite to eat. The waitress asked if they wanted red or green chili. The only chili Polly was familiar with were the little hot yellow peppers that came in a jar. Polly and Peggy were totally unfamiliar with chili, a commodity no native New Mexican could live without. Polly wasn't partial to spicy food so she passed on the chili.

After breakfast, the girls decided to check out the town that would be their home for awhile. It seemed nice enough. It was a desert town nestled amidst rugged peaks. They saw a lot of cacti and a few bushes but not much else. The weather was really hot and reminded Polly of the Texas town where they had gone on vacation.

A few days after their arrival, the keys to the motel were in Polly's hands. She was now the new manager of the Super 8 Motel in Las Cruces, New Mexico. When she had worked up enough nerve to call Walt, she told him she had accepted the job of managing a motel in New Mexico. When she told him it was in Las Cruces, he bellowed, "Where in the hell is Las

Cruces?" She replied that she wasn't exactly sure except that it was a very long way from Pierre, South Dakota. She told him it had been such a long trip that she thought they would never reach New Mexico. He asked why she had left town without a word to him about her intentions. Walt said, "You caught me completely off guard! How could you do this to me? I would never leave you the way you left me without a clue and no warning!"

Walt had evidently fallen madly in love with Polly, and even though Polly cared very much for Walt, she didn't love him in that way. She told him she was sorry but at the time it seemed the only way. At first, Walt called her every day asking when she was coming home. She told him she didn't think she would ever be returning to Pierre. There was dead silence except for the pounding of Walt's heart.

Polly felt horrible about the way she had treated Walt. She immersed herself in her work to keep from dealing with the guilt she felt. She wondered if she had made a mistake by not accepting his proposal of marriage, but it was too late for second thoughts. Las Cruces was a long way from South Dakota and it would be really difficult for Walt to visit her. Polly had made her decision, and knew she had to make a new life for herself without Walt. Life without Walt would not be easy because she cared very deeply for him and he was madly in love with her. He had even offered to move to New Mexico just to be with her.

CHAPTER 25

Polly was doing really well financially, and decided to purchase a house in Las Cruces. Walt eventually moved in with Polly. Since he was working as a pilot for Southwest Airlines, it wasn't difficult for him to transfer from Pierre, South Dakota to Las Cruces, New Mexico.

Everything was going so well in Las Cruces that Polly's bosses informed her she would be going to Georgia to open a new motel. She told them that whenever they were ready she was up to the challenge.

Meantime, Polly and Walt were trying very hard to make their relationship work. Walt wanted to marry her, but Polly wasn't ready for such a permanent commitment. They had a great sexual relationship and he catered to her every whim, but she didn't love him in the same way that he loved her. Polly was still scarred by her first marriage. She wasn't ready to try it again.

Walt was desperately in love with Polly. He tried every way he knew to convince her to marry him. His attempts were futile and their relationship was at a stalemate. One morning, as they were having coffee and getting ready for work, Polly told Walt that if he was so miserable he should go back to South Dakota. The following afternoon, with a heavy heart, Walt did just that. With Walt gone, Polly immersed herself in her work even more. Walt continued to call her every now and then.

In her position, Polly met new people every day. Once in a while, she and Peggy would go to Juárez, Mexico and party. Everything was less expensive in Juárez, so the girls would shop at the *mercados*. Polly and Peggy bought liquor in Juárez because it was a lot cheaper. They then crossed the border into El Paso, Texas where they partied all night, bar hopping to meet men. The next morning both girls would be back at work. They were really having a good time. They liked their jobs and they also loved to party. They met a lot of men in the bars in Las Cruces. One of their favorite pastimes was playing pool.

Polly's boss called and told her that she had been assigned to open a new motel in Truckee, California. The company jet flew her from Las Cruces to Reno, Nevada, where a limousine was waiting to take her to the site where the new motel was being built. Most of the construction had already been finished. Polly's headquarters for the duration of her stay in California had been completed and furnished. It was mid-afternoon when she arrived. The weather was hot, but not as hot as Las Cruces. There was a lot of activity going on as Polly surveyed the area. One of the crews was building a swimming pool while another crew laid asphalt. A jackhammer could be heard as preparations were being made for the pouring of concrete where the sidewalks would be located. Polly was impressed by the industriousness of the workers. She remembered her experience with the previous contractor, and she prayed this one would show a little more respect for her authority. As was the case in Farmington, Polly knew many men resented having a woman in charge, but like it or not, she was the boss and they would have to learn to accept it. It wasn't Polly's style to lord it over her subordinates.

As soon as she settled in, she walked over to the construction foreman's trailer to introduce herself. Polly walked into the trailer, and a man sitting behind a desk asked if he could help her. She told him her name was Polly Laffrenzen, she was the representative for the Super 8 Motels, and she would like to speak to the foreman. The man behind the desk was in his early thirties with blond hair and the deepest blue eyes she had ever seen. He picked up the phone, dialed a number, and spoke to someone on the other end of the line. When he hung up the phone, he told Polly the foreman would see her, and directed her to the rear of the trailer.

Polly knocked on the door of what appeared to be an office and waited for a reply. After a moment, a male voice asked her to enter. In the room was a short man smoking a big cigar. His messy desk was full of papers. He spoke in a soft voice and had noticeably yellow teeth, especially when he smiled. He asked Polly, "How may I help you, Ma'am?" She replied, "I am Polly Laffrenzen, the representative of Super 8 Motel. I'm here to open the new motel." He asked Polly to please have a seat. She sat on a chair that was just as dusty as everything else in the office.

Polly asked the foreman, whose name was Joe Gibbs, how much longer it would be before she could take over the motel so she could get it ready for the Grand Opening. He told her it would take a couple more months before construction was completed. To her relief, Polly got along really well with Joe, which would make her job that much easier. He was easygoing, well mannered, and a natural born comedian.

That night, Polly and some of the guys from the crew drove to Reno to have dinner, do a little gambling, and see a few shows at the casinos. These guys were great, and Polly got along with them too. They got so drunk that night that they had to help each other to their cars. As drunk as they were, it was a miracle they made it back to Truckee without incident. The next day they were all suffering massive hangovers. It turned out to be a really long day. After work, Polly and the same bunch of guys headed to a local bar to try and cure their horrible hangovers. They played pool, which had become Polly's favorite pastime. She was good at it too! She would only play for money: nothing less than twenty dollars a game. She won most of the games. It seemed that the more liquored up she got, the better she played. These guys respected her, though, and she appreciated it.

They were lousy pool players, and Polly was taking them for all they had because she had mastered the game of pool. Being a woman helped because she had a way of teasing her opponent, which gave her the edge. She distracted him with a mesmerizing smile that worked like a charm. Polly loved winning!

Again, they stayed out late and got stinking drunk. Even though they were hung over the next morning, they didn't let it slow them down.

Polly interviewed some of the local people for the various positions at the Super 8 Motel. She needed desk clerks, maintenance people, maids, etc. She hired a couple to help her decorate the rooms. Eighteen-wheelers would regularly stop in front of the motel loaded with furniture for the motel. Corporate headquarters always ordered the best.

There was never a dull moment in Polly's life these days. She kept herself very busy, and when he found out where she was stationed, Walt would call her, and they spent hours talking on the phone. He never failed to ask when she planned on returning to Pierre. She would honestly reply that she didn't think she would ever go back because the Super 8 Motel Corporation was expanding, which meant the construction of a motel in a different location every eighteen days. Polly loved her job and thrived on the challenge.

Truckee, a small town, was not in the least bit boring. One night, after Polly and a few of the workers went to play pool, have a few drinks, and do a little dancing, the foreman was thrown in jail for drinking and driving. Polly had to bail him out. Partying after work had become a ritual. Polly liked the idea that everyone seemed to get along quite well, which made her job that much easier.

Decorating the motel rooms was a demanding job for Polly, a fanatical perfectionist. If a room didn't turn out to her complete satisfaction, she would redo it. Polly's penchant for being so meticulous drove some of her employees crazy. Everything had to be done to her specifications.

After the motel was completed and the employees properly trained, Polly returned to Las Cruces. The day that she left Truckee everyone was teary-eyed. They had become friends with Polly and didn't want her to leave. But she was one of Super 8 Motel's highest paid employees, and there was no place in Truckee that could come close to paying her that kind of money.

Polly was beginning to like the idea of traveling from town to town. She marveled at the difference in local customs as well as personalities as she traveled throughout the U.S. The company jet flew Polly back to Las Cruces, where Peggy was waiting for her. Both girls were delighted to see each other again. Polly had been gone six months and Peggy had missed her terribly.

Peggy and Polly sat waiting for the arrival of new guests. As they waited, Polly related her varied experiences to Peggy. She told her about the things she had done, the places she had been, and the people she had met – especially the men. Even though Truckee was a town Polly wouldn't soon forget, she was glad to be back in Las Cruces. She couldn't help but wonder how long it would be before she was sent on another assignment. She loved the motel business. The variety of people she met in her capacity as representative of the Super 8 Motel was astounding. She dealt with people from all walks of life and at different economic and social levels.

Polly had been in Las Cruces for only a couple of weeks when she was notified that she was being sent to Georgia to open another Super 8 Motel. She was so sure that she'd be given a new assignment she hadn't even bothered to unpack.

As Polly was flown to her new destination, she thought about how happy and content she was with her new life. She thought, 'It can't get any better than this.' She loved the attention, the prestige, and the money.

When she arrived in Macon, Georgia, her bosses were there to greet her. As she got off the plane she was hit by the intense heat and humidity. This had to be the hottest place she'd been to yet. She could even feel her makeup melting.

Her bosses took her in a limousine to an exclusive restaurant for lunch. It was a business lunch, and the conversation centered on the destiny of the company. They were very pleased at the progress thus far, and the fact that most of the motels had been completed right on schedule. Everything was moving along far better than they had expected. Their goal was to have a Super 8 Motel constructed in every town across America by the year 1990. It sounded far-fetched but Polly sat there taking it all in. Their optimistic projections were music to her ears because she knew that, as long as they kept building their motels, her future was secure. She liked the fact that she could put most of her earnings in the bank. Polly believed very strongly in saving money for a "rainy day", and her job allowed her to do just that.

After the meeting, Polly rented a room at a motel close to the Super 8 Motel so she could keep an eye on the progress of its construction. The completion of this Super 8 Motel seemed to be a long way off. Polly knew she had gotten there much too soon because it would be a couple of months before the motel was completed. She anticipated a very boring wait.

The heat was unbearable. She located the foreman in charge of the construction and introduced herself. He appeared to be in his forties and was quite handsome. He also seemed to be of Irish descent and spoke with a deep Southern accent. He had a mouthful of chewing tobacco and a serious look on his face. From his demeanor, Polly pegged him as a no-nonsense type of guy. She asked him how long he thought it would take to complete the job. He told her it would be at least a couple of months because the material he had ordered had not arrived yet, but was expected shortly.

As he accompanied her to her motel, he asked if she would like to have lunch after she got settled in. Polly replied, "I'd love to." When she arrived at her motel room, she decided to take a much-needed nap as she was experiencing the effects of jet lag. She was so exhausted that she slept till the following morning, when she was awakened by a knock on her door. When she opened the door, she saw Jake Summers, the construction foreman, standing there. He invited her to breakfast. She accepted his invitation but told him he would have to give her an hour to get ready. After he left, she took a bath, put on some makeup and got dressed.

When Jake returned within the hour to pick Polly up, he couldn't help but notice how beautiful Polly looked. Jake had been married for over twenty years until cancer claimed his wife's life. He had been left with two children to raise on his own. He was totally bereft at the death of his wife of twenty years. He didn't think he could go on without her, yet he knew he had to be strong for the sake of his children. He was fortunate to have his mother living nearby so that he could continue working. His mother adored her grandchildren, which gave Jake the opportunity to immerse himself in his work in an effort to cope with his tremendous loss.

Until he met Polly, Jake's work was his life. He was lonely, but he hadn't met anyone he really cared for. Polly, however, awakened in Jake feelings that had remained dormant since his wife's death. She had a way about her that intrigued him. She was soft and feminine, yet he sensed an inner strength and intelligence that intrigued him.

They had brunch at a small diner where everybody seemed to know Jake. Polly was impressed by his apparent popularity. Even the waitresses were on a first name basis with him. When they were finished eating, Jake gave Polly a tour of Macon. It was a beautiful town. It had a large variety of fabulous flowers and trees. The town was very well maintained and free of litter. Jake asked Polly if she had ever seen the ocean, to which she replied, "No." He asked if she would like to visit the ocean on the weekend, and she said yes.

Friday after work, Jake picked Polly up at her motel, where she was anxiously waiting for him. She was wearing a light blue low-cut blouse, a pair of blue denim shorts, and white sandals. She wore her hair up with spiraling curls. She was always very meticulous about applying her makeup. It was a warm evening but not as hot as the day had been.

They encountered heavy traffic as they headed towards North Carolina. Everyone seemed in a hurry to get someplace. It was an eight-hour drive to the Carolina shores. When they arrived, the sun was coming up from the east. Polly had never seen anything as beautiful as the ocean. They took their shoes off and walked along the beach. The sand felt wonderful under their feet. As they walked along the beach, the warmth of the sun made Polly feel glad to be alive.

Life's unpredictability never ceased to amaze Polly. When she accepted this assignment, she had no idea she would meet a man like Jake. The mutual attraction was electrifying. They sat near some rocks where they could hear the waves of the ocean crashing against the rock wall. In all her travels Polly had never seen an ocean, and she was astounded by its vastness. She was so intrigued by what she was experiencing that she lost all track of time. When they resumed their walk along the beach, Polly began picking up seashells that she found along the way. They were having so much fun that for awhile, time seemed to stand still.

By noon they were famished and decided to get something to eat. They rented a motel room nearby so they could shower before returning to the beach, where they spent the rest of the day. Polly cautiously walked towards the water just far enough to get her feet wet. The water was a bit chilly but it didn't take long to get used to it. They even built a sandcastle. Polly and Jake were having a really good time together. Seeing the ocean was something Polly had never even thought about. Yet here she was with a devastatingly handsome man building sandcastles and collecting seashells.

To top off their marvelous day at the beach, Jake took Polly dancing. Unfortunately, all good things come to an end. Jake escorted Polly to her motel room and returned to his own room. That night, their thoughts were so full of all the wonderful events of the day and the time they had spent together that neither one got much sleep.

The following morning they were up at the crack of dawn. After breakfast they drove to a beach located in a different part of North Carolina. It was a very pleasant drive filled with exquisitely beautiful sights. Polly drank it all in. She told Jake she was having the most wonderful time, and would love to do it again. It had been a very busy weekend, and she wanted to savor every glorious moment. The experience was like something out of a storybook. This was one of those precious memories that Polly stored in her heart and mind along with all her other unforgettable and wonderful memories.

On Sunday, they drove back to Georgia. It was a weekend that Polly wouldn't soon forget. Jake promised to take her to the beach again. From then on, she and Jake were good friends.

Polly anxiously waited for the Super 8 Motel to be completed. Progress was slow. The biggest setback was their inability to acquire the materials they needed to complete the job. The wait was very frustrating. Polly wasn't used to being idle. Her bosses had blundered by sending her out too soon, since the motel was still a long way from being finished.

She entertained herself by acquainting herself with the town. She would walk around sightseeing, go to the local bars, have a few drinks, and play pool. Polly was the type of woman who without even trying invariably attracted men. Polly, however, was not interested in their attentions. She was there to play pool and that's all!

A month went by and the motel was still far from completed. Polly and Jake continued to date. In the evening, when Jake got off work, he would take Polly on long drives out to the country to show her the beauty that abounded in Georgia. The evening rains served to cool the hot days. The humidity was at times unbearable, making a person feel sweaty and sticky.

Jake and Polly went back to the beach in North Carolina and had as much fun as they had the first time they were there. Polly loved the ocean, and was captivated by its vastness and power. Jake had been marvelously attentive and had shown her something she had never experienced before. She had thought she was moving into the "world" when she moved to

Minneapolis, but now she was acutely aware that there was so much more she had to discover and so many new people she had yet to meet.

After spending another weekend on the beaches of North Carolina, they returned to Georgia to a motel that was still incomplete. Polly was disappointed because she hated sitting around waiting.

But the day finally came when the contractors turned the motel over to Polly so she could start hiring the personnel necessary to run the motel. This was the part of her job that Polly loved. She enjoyed meeting people and holding interviews. She didn't like turning people away, but there were only so many positions she could fill.

When her job was completed, Polly returned to Las Cruces. She had been there a week when Walt decided to visit her. He proposed marriage to her again, and again she refused. She had been down that road before, and chose not to travel it again. Since her divorce she had met many eligible men. A lot of them had very appealing qualities and would probably make good husbands, but having experienced twenty-five years of marriage, Polly liked her life just the way it was, with no permanent attachments and the freedom to do as she pleased. She loved her job as well as her independence.

Polly loved Walt, but not with the intensity that he loved her. She still felt bad about the fact that at one time he had left Pierre, South Dakota, leaving everything behind just to be with her. Polly sympathized with him and wished things could be different, but they weren't, and Walt would just have to accept it or spend the rest of his life pining for her. As Walt boarded the flight that would take him back to Pierre, his heart was aching so badly he just wanted to die rather than face life without Polly. Polly prayed that by some miracle he would get over her and get on with his life.

Polly's next assignment took her to Hobbs, New Mexico where she was to open another Super 8 Motel. To her chagrin, she ran into the same obstacle that had made her job in Farmington such a pain. The contractor turned out to be a real asshole and a pompous know-it-all, and Polly's new assignment proved to be a nightmare. Everything seemed to be going wrong. She was totally frustrated and couldn't see the light at the end of the tunnel. Because of the problems, her bosses requested that she keep them informed of any and all obstacles she encountered. Things got so bad that company headquarters sent the manager from South Dakota. Polly had to train him. He was thirty-five years old and quite handsome. Polly had become a good judge of character because of her many experiences, and didn't trust him. There was something about him she didn't like, but she trained him, since she had been instructed to do so by the company. This guy reminded her of a gigolo she had once met in Minneapolis.

After Polly completed the hiring of employees who would be running the motel in Hobbs, she was sent back to Las Cruces. She was beginning to like Las Cruces. When she wasn't working she played pool with some of the locals. She was developing a reputation as an excellent pool player. The guys liked to give her a hard time because they had never met a woman who could play pool as well as Polly. Peggy was also becoming adept at pool.

<h1 style="text-align:center"><u>CHAPTER 26</u></h1>

One day, Polly received a phone call from her brother informing her that her mother had died. She dropped the phone and screamed in shock. She could feel an intense pain in her heart, as if it were literally breaking. She began to weep hysterically, and couldn't stop crying for hours after she received the painful news. She loved her mother so much, but hadn't realized just how much until now, when she was gone forever. The pain in her heart was unbearable as she cried out loud, "Mamma, I love you! Please don't be dead! You can't be gone, Mamma. I still need you in my life!"

Her mother had been very protective of her ever since she was a little girl. She had always made her wear those large red bows on her head so that people driving cars could see her from a distance – her mother's way of protecting her from getting run over. Polly recalled the day she painted the dogs pink for the town parade. She had so many memories of all the wonderful times she and her mother had shared. Now she was gone, and Polly hadn't had the chance to say "Goodbye" or a final "I love you". Polly felt a pain that wouldn't go away.

Polly had been fortunate to have two loving and caring parents. Now they were both gone, along with her grandparents. She felt hopelessly alone and helpless. Intellectually she knew her mother was dead, but psychologically she found the reality very difficult to accept. In her mind's eye she could still see her mother as she had looked when Polly was a little girl. Such wonderful memories of her childhood flooded Polly's mind. She recalled the cold winter nights when the wind was howling and it had snowed for a couple of days. They would sit around the fireplace drinking hot chocolate and listening to their grandmother's stories about the old country. They were such wonderful stories. Thoughts of her grandmother brought renewed tears. Her mother was her final link to a childhood she cherished, and with her passing away the connection had disappeared. She knew life would never be the same again.

As the memories continued to flood her mind, the pain of loss became much worse. She remembered the good times she had enjoyed when she lived at home. Lillian, her mother, would cook the best foods for Polly's country parties. All of Polly's friends loved Lillian. She was a good wife, a wonderful mother, and a remarkable woman. Polly knew that Lillian's greatest pride was her son Sonny. Even though she knew that Sonny was Lillian's "favorite", she was never jealous. Polly loved her brother very much.

The tears and the memories continued to flood her, as did the pain. Peggy checked on Polly to make sure she was okay. Because they were best friends, they laughed and cried as Polly shared some of her memories with Peggy.

The next day, Polly flew back to Pipestone, Minnesota to attend her mother's funeral. Throughout the years Polly had attended her class reunions, which served to maintain the link between Polly and her former classmates. Polly and most of her classmates had remained good friends.

When Polly got back to Pipestone, most of her friends stopped by the farm to offer their condolences. When her former girlfriends stopped by, Polly couldn't hold back the tears. She still found it unfathomable that her mother was dead. When she saw Lillian in the coffin, reality hit her and she broke down, crying hysterically. Her eyes were red and swollen from all the tears she had shed. She didn't know what she was going to do without her mother. Whenever she'd been down, the first thing she did was call her mother and tell her her problems. Lillian always gave her sage advice. Now that her mother was gone, she had no one to turn to who loved her so unconditionally.

Polly was so devastated by her mother's death that she couldn't eat or sleep. Her friends tried to console her, but to no avail. She would lie on her bed in her room staring into space, realizing what an intricate part of her life her mother had been. She could actually hear her mother's voice echoing in the house, saying, "Polly, get up. It's time to go to school. Hurry up because I still have to put your bow on." Little Polly would hurry so that her mother could put on her bow. In her mind's eye she could see her father at the kitchen table drinking coffee and Sonny eating breakfast. Such wonderful memories! The realization dawned on Polly that after all is said and done, memories are all we have left. Polly had no idea how she could face the rest of her life without her mother.

The day of her mother's funeral was the saddest and darkest day in Polly's life. As her mother was being buried, Polly went into shock. She cried so hard she made herself sick. As she wept she cried out to her mother, "Mamma, come back to me! I miss you too much! I love you with all my heart!"

When Polly returned to Las Cruces, she was still feeling the sorrow of her mother's death. The trauma of her loss consumed her thoughts, and in the days that followed she found it very difficult to concentrate on her work. Her mother's face was constantly on her mind. Without warning, tears would stream down her face and her throat would tighten. It took a very long time for the pain of her loss to ease up. The thought of never seeing her mother again haunted her ceaselessly. As always, whenever Polly was in pain, she immersed herself in her work. The pain of losing her mother was so intense that she had to double her efforts to lose herself in her work.

Polly was sent back to Hobbs because of some managerial problems. The manager was tapping the till and not making deposits on time. He was embezzling money from the company. As soon as Polly arrived in Hobbs, the manager, Bob, was relieved of his position as manager. It was Polly's responsibility to straighten everything out and hire a new manager to run the motel. A few days after the manager was relieved of his duties, Polly was working the desk when a gunman disguised with a mask walked into the motel and told Polly, "Give me all your money or I'll shoot you!" Polly started laughing because she knew it was Bob. He was wearing the same socks he had worn the day before. Polly told him that if he was going to rob her, he should at least have had enough sense to change his socks. As she stood there laughing, Bob got angry and walked out without a penny. Polly stood there not believing his stupidity.

After awhile, it hit Polly. She could have been shot! She began to shake as she thought, 'My God, I could have been shot! The gall of that man! What was that heel thinking coming in here and pointing a gun at me! The son-of-a-bitch must be plain loco to attempt something so stupid!' She called the company and reported the incident to her boss. She was told to send Bob back to Aberdeen, South Dakota and they would take care of the situation.

After Polly sent Bob back to Aberdeen, she began looking for a suitable manager to replace Bob, who had traded rooms for favors and did whatever he wanted without caring whether the company made any money. He was a greedy little guy who cared for no one but himself. It took Polly a couple of weeks before she got the books in order and some profit began to show. She hired the head of housekeeping and her husband to be the new managers. She had encountered as many problems in Hobbs as she had in Farmington. There wasn't even a decent bar in Hobbs. She spent a couple more weeks training the new managers.

From Hobbs, New Mexico she was sent to Columbus, Georgia to open another Super 8 Motel. Traveling was her favorite part of her job. New Super 8's were popping up in every part of the United States. Her bosses were very rich. These motels were being built as fast as the construction companies could build them, and she was more than eager to tackle them all.

Columbus, Georgia was a lot like Brunswick, Georgia. At least they had a few decent bars where she could play a game of pool. One of Polly's most amazing traits was the ease with which she made friends regardless of the locale. She not only had the knack of easily acquiring new friends, she was also a "male magnet". Whenever she felt the urge, she would pick up a total stranger and indulge in sexual escapades. What frustrated her was that after only a couple of dates the men began talking marriage. It really bothered her, since "marriage" was not part of her vocabulary. Most of the men she met were just friends.

Polly loved the green lushness of Georgia. The country around Columbus had a lot of rolling hills and an abundance of trees. It was a military town. Fort Benning was where Airborne Rangers and most of the Army's elite were trained. It was basically a G.I. town. After serving their time in the Army, many of the soldiers decided to make it their home, which accounted for its steady growth. Construction was heavy along Highway 185.

Once Polly's mission of hiring the managers for the Super 8 Motel in Columbus was completed, the company's Lear jet was sent to pick her up. The pilot and Polly had become good friends. He rented a car and went to the motel to pick Polly up. They decided to have a beer at a local tavern and play some pool before leaving Columbus. They couldn't decide what to drink, so Polly suggested Foster's Australian Beer. The pilot had always wanted to try one, so he agreed and they ordered. Before they realized it, they were on their third beer and feeling no pain. They drank a few more beers and played some pool. Both of them got smashed, and couldn't remember driving back to the motel. Polly miraculously made it to her room, and the pilot stayed in one of the other rooms.

The following morning the pilot had such a bad hangover there was no way he could fly the Lear Jet, so they stayed in Columbus an extra day. They then flew to Aberdeen, South Dakota for a big company meeting. The discussion centered on the location for a new Super 8 Motel. Officers Ron Rivit and Dennis Brown were clueless on the management of a motel. Polly did all the leg work and research. Polly loved the motel business and had become an invaluable asset to the company. They valued and respected Polly's intuitiveness, and listened to any advice and suggestions Polly offered.

A few days after the company meeting, Polly was sent to Crystal Lake, Illinois. The motel that was being built there was nearing completion. She was flown to her destination by the same pilot who had picked her up in Columbus, Georgia. When they saw each other, they began to laugh as they remembered how drunk they had gotten just a few nights before. Polly jokingly asked him if he would like to do it again. He replied he'd have to pass because the memory of his horrendous hangover was still too fresh in his memory.

The Super 8 Motel in Crystal Lake was being built near a lake in a ritzy part of town. Everything was very plush, and elegant houses adorned the area. Polly was impressed with the beautiful houses and classy neighborhood. Within a few days of her arrival, Polly took over the motel from the contractors and began hiring the employees that would run the motel. Everything went quite smoothly. She wished it could have been this easy in all the other places she had worked.

The manager she had hired to run the Super 8 Motel in Crystal Lake appeared wearing a double-breasted suit and carrying a brief case. Polly told her she had better change clothes because they had a lot of rooms to clean before the Grand Opening. They also had to advertise the Grand Opening in the local newspapers and radio station. There was a lot of work to be done. After much physical as well as promotional work, the motel was ready for opening day. Many local businessmen stopped by to welcome them to Crystal Lake. Polly stuck around a few extra days to make sure the manager she had hired was capable of running the motel.

While working in the office one day, Polly met a nice man named Kimbal, who was a consultant engineer. They hit it off right away. Not being shy, he asked Polly if he could show her around town. She accepted his invitation, and they drove around Lake Michigan. It was breathtaking. He drove her into Chicago. She was impressed with all the tall buildings in downtown Chicago. It was a fabulous city. The season was beginning to change, and leaves were changing color and the weather was beginning to get chilly. It was a sure indication that winter would soon be here, when the wind chill factor dropped below zero and it would get frigidly cold. The winters in this part of the country were just like in Minnesota.

As they drove around, Polly was enthralled by the buildings and the people as well as the scenery. Kimbal proved to be a perfect gentleman. When the evening was over, he took her back to the motel and didn't make a pass at her. She thanked him for a wonderful day, and they parted company.

When she was back in her room, she called Peggy to see how she was doing. Polly told her she missed her and looked forward to seeing her again. Peggy was alone in Las Cruces. It had been quite a while since Polly had left Las Cruces, and she told Peggy she wouldn't be back any time soon. She told Peggy she was going to Nyack, New York and didn't know when she would be returning to Las Cruces. Peggy advised Polly to be careful in her travels. Polly told her not to worry, that she would be just fine.

Polly found the people in Nyack unfriendly. The motel was as yet incomplete and she knew she would be there awhile. She knew her stay in Nyack would be lonely. But Polly wasn't one to wallow in self-pity, and she always enjoyed the unexpected. Nyack was approximately 45 miles from New York City. Polly had always wanted to see New York City.

Finally the motel was finished and her part of the job began. She began interviewing and hiring the people who would staff the motel. Competent help was not easy to find. The day they were ready to put out all the linen, they discovered it had been stolen. Polly went into a state of panic for awhile, not knowing how she was going to replace that much linen. She called some of the other motels in the area asking if they had extra linen she could buy from them until she could get a new shipment. The Grand Opening was scheduled for the following day, a Friday. People were already making reservations for the weekend. Most of them just wanted to escape New York City for the weekend.

Undaunted, Polly shopped at the local stores, buying whatever linen they had in stock. Most of the people were very rude, and Polly kept thinking, 'I've got to get the heck out of this town and go back to Las Cruces where people are nice.' Nyack needed an attitude adjustment. It hadn't been easy, but she had finally acquired all the linen she needed for the opening of the motel.

The last few weeks had been rough. She had never felt so lonely and alone. All she could think about was going home. She had come to consider Las Cruces her home.

On opening day, every room in the motel had been rented to African-Americans who wanted to get out of New York City for the weekend. In the days that followed, things improved around the motel. No more linen was stolen.

Early one morning, Polly met a truck driver who seemed like a very nice person. They carried on a conversation as if they had known each other for years. She told him that she had always wanted to see New York City. He told her, "I'll take you to New York City if you want to go." She responded, "Let's go! I need to get out of this place for a couple of days anyway." Polly got ready while he was busy unhooking his big tractor-trailer. Within a few minutes they were on the New York Turnpike heading towards the city. The traffic was manic. Everybody seemed in an awful hurry to get somewhere.

Slim, the truck driver, was in his late forties. He had been driving trucks for more than twenty years. He had a very outgoing personality and was rather handsome, and it was obvious he kept his body in good shape. Apparently Slim was used to crazy traffic because he put the pedal to the metal and made it to New York City in half an hour. There were a few times when Polly wondered if she would make it to New York City alive.

When Polly saw the skyline of New York City, she was awed by its grandiosity. The pictures she had seen in books did not do it justice. They exited the freeway and drove into town, where she saw large crowds of people. In her entire life, Polly had never seen so many different people gathered in one place. There were tall ones, short ones, skinny ones, fat ones, and all of various ethnic backgrounds; it was amazing. Polly was impressed by the stylishly dressed women and the men in their three-piece business suits.

Slim parked the truck, and he and Polly joined the hordes of people who filled the sidewalks of New York City. It was a concrete jungle. Everyone seemed to be in a great hurry to get somewhere. Polly gazed up at the tall buildings. As she peered into the store windows, she was dazzled by the stylish clothes on display. Clothes had always been her number one love, and she had been considered a trendsetter in Pipestone.

As she window-shopped, Polly decided to buy some of the beautiful clothes she saw for herself. She was having a great time window-shopping. Never had she seen such a great array of fashion on display. New York City was considered the fashion and glamour capitol of the world. This visit was the ultimate high for Polly. From what she witnessed, she thought the "fashion god" must live in New York City. She was surrounded by people who exuded style and sophistication. Polly felt out of her element amongst such high-class people.

As the silent elite paraded past Polly, she could smell the scent of expensive perfume. They reminded her of shadows passing each other without giving or expecting acknowledgment. Polly was awed by the hustle and bustle of life in this big city. The streets were filled with Yellow Cabs picking up and dropping off fares. Over eight million people were on the move, apparently accustomed to, and oblivious of their surroundings.

Polly and Slim visited the Statue of Liberty and Rockefeller Center. They strolled through Central Park "people-watching". As they observed the people in Central Park they couldn't help but notice the contrast from what they had seen in the affluent part of New York City. In Central Park there were people who looked like they hadn't eaten in several days or bathed for months. They also saw joggers, people walking their dogs, and others just enjoying an afternoon stroll through the Park.

That evening, Polly and Slim dined in a small restaurant near the Park. Polly was famished. She hadn't had anything to eat all day. As much as Polly loved the hustle and bustle of New York City, she definitely wouldn't want to live there. The pace was much too fast for her taste. She enjoyed the slower lifestyle and friendliness of people in a smaller town. She had thoroughly enjoyed her exciting visit to the "Big Apple" and knew it was an experience she would not soon forget, but in her heart she was just a small-town girl.

The trip back to Nyack seemed to take much longer than the trip into New York City. On the way back to Nyack, Polly ruminated on the many adventures of their day. It had been wonderful. She was exhausted but happy. When they got back to the motel, Polly thanked Slim for the exciting day. Slim told her he had had a great time too, and he would be heading for California in the morning. They parted company and Polly headed for her room. By the time her head hit the pillow it was midnight.

She could hardly wait to tell Peggy how marvelous and fascinating New York City was. The most intriguing part of her adventures in the "Big Apple" had been the fashions. Polly loved beautiful clothes, and had never seen such a fantastic collection of chic fashions like the ones in New York City. Uppermost in her thoughts was that if she ever became a millionaire, she would buy the finest things money could buy.

Polly not only had style and class, she also had the determination and tenacity to make her dreams come true. Polly had started with nothing, and had worked very hard to make something of herself. Despite many setbacks, Polly had become quite independent and was pleased with her life at that moment. She would not trade it for anything in the world. Her bosses were great and the money was good. Life was good!

She waited around a few days in Nyack because they had another motel almost ready for opening. Nyack was not her kind of town. They didn't accept outsiders. A few days later, company headquarters called her and told her to rent a car and drive to Danbury, Connecticut. She made the trip to Connecticut, where a new motel had already been built. The manager had quit, and the assistant manager had taken over. He was from South Dakota. When Polly arrived, he explained to her that his wife was expecting their first child and he wanted to be there with her. The following morning he left for Pierre, South Dakota.

Polly had to change all the locks because the manager had taken the motel keys with him, and it made her very nervous. The manager had also left the place in a shambles. Polly had her work cut out for her, organizing everything and making sure the motel met her high standards. The motel in Danbury was in a real rough neighborhood that Polly didn't like.

CHAPTER 27

Polly had been away from home a long time and was getting very homesick. She missed the people and the delicious New Mexico green chili.

The following week, Polly flew out of Newark, New Jersey and headed for El Paso, where Peggy met her. They were both overjoyed to see each other again. They had been apart for much too long! They decided to have some fun and party in Juárez, Mexico.

They went bar hopping and indulged in some serious drinking. Everywhere they went the Mexican men tried to pick them up because they were both very attractive blondes with great figures. They flirted a little, but mostly they wanted to enjoy each other's company. As they walked from bar to bar, people tried to sell them a sundry assortment of goods, including drugs. The girls felt sorry for the street beggars and handed them dollar bills. Polly felt especially bad for the children, and gave them money hoping it would buy them something to eat. Despite the professional hustlers, there were genuinely poor people begging on the streets, and they touched the women's hearts.

One of the bars they entered was very dark. Rock and roll music blared. On stage a young Mexican girl was dancing to the beat of the music. Her moves were fluid and erotic. The American soldiers who were there were whistling and being quite boisterous. Most of these soldiers were far from home. They whooped and hollered as the cute Mexican girl danced. In Juárez a guy could get drunk and laid for very little money.

Polly and Peggy had a few drinks before they left to find a bar that wasn't so rowdy. When they were through bar hopping, they crossed the border to the United States. They were both half-looped as they drove back to Las Cruces. Polly had begun to feel the effects of jet lag.

When they arrived back at the motel, Polly took a long hot bath. Relaxing in the tub helped her sleep better. Later that night she got a call from Walt proclaiming his love. He said he wanted to return to Las Cruces to be with her. She told him it was okay with her. She was still in love with Walt. He was not only a wonderful man, but he was also very good to Polly. They had shared many wonderful times together. There was nothing Walt wouldn't do for Polly. He was madly in love with her and worshiped the ground she walked on.

Polly met him at the airport in El Paso. She was never so happy to see anyone in her life. She rushed into his arms and kissed him with great passion. They held onto each other for a long while. Her heart was racing as he held her close.

After they left the airport, they drove to a restaurant and had lunch. They filled each other in on what had been going on in their lives since they had last seen each other. For the past few months Polly had been very lonely. She needed Walt in her life right now to make her feel like a woman again. When they returned to the motel, Walt and Polly made love with enormous passion. He wanted to fulfill her every need. They spent the rest of the day making love. When they were both satisfied, they fell asleep in each other's arms.

The following morning, when they awoke, they were still holding on to each other, and they realized it had not been a dream. They made love again before they got up and showered together. Afterward they went to a local café for a bite to eat. It had been a long time since Polly had felt so happy. They wanted very much to be together, so Walt moved back to Las Cruces. They were both happier than they had been in a long time.

Walt got a job as a pilot with Southwest Airlines. He flew Lear jets – mainly private corporate planes. On one of his trips to California, he asked Polly to accompany him. When she agreed, Walt was elated. Polly made him feel complete, and Polly felt the same way about Walt. She was totally in love with him. Whenever they flew somewhere, their passengers were always very important people. They flew these VIPs to different parts of the country. Polly enjoyed flying with Walt. It was also a good way for her to see America. Polly and Walt dined at some of the finest restaurants in the many cities they visited.

Even though home base was Las Cruces, New Mexico, her new assignment was in Pensacola, Florida. Polly's spirits were low the day she left for Florida. She and Walt had been getting along so well, and now they had to face a separation neither one was looking forward to.

The company Lear Jet flew Polly to a Pensacola motel that was experiencing a few problems. Polly was a troubleshooter and had been sent to resolve them. When they arrived in Florida, they encountered a pounding rainstorm that didn't look as if it was going to let up any time soon. As she traveled from the airport to the motel, rivers of rain ran down the streets and flooded the sidewalks. She had seen snow, but not much rain. She thought to herself, 'Rain, rain, go away. Come again some other day.' It was apparently monsoon season, and the force of the rain was beating the roof shingles of the motel. The torrential downpour was at its peak. Polly was not at all impressed with Pensacola. Something about the place gave her an eerie feeling.

The following day, the head of housekeeping summoned her to one of the rooms. She had something she wanted to show her. Polly asked one of the other girls to watch the office while she went to see what was going on. A group of maids was standing outside Room 113. They looked distraught about something. When Polly entered the room, she noticed a pool of blood on the bed covered with a towel. What Polly saw next was one of the most gruesome sights she had ever witnessed in her life. When she removed the towel she saw a fetus. Evidently a woman had aborted her unborn child and just left it there. Polly found it to be one of the most unconscionable abominations she had ever witnessed. The poor infant had been left for someone else to dispose of. At the very least, this little angel deserved a proper burial. Polly couldn't begin to understand what kind of woman would be capable of such an atrocious act. Polly called the authorities and reported her findings. The atmosphere in the motel was subdued and somber for the next few days.

During their investigation all the police could come up with was that the room had been rented to a woman who had used an alias. They never determined who the child had belonged to.

A few days after finding the fetus, Polly called the room of one of the guests to find out if he would be staying another night. There was no answer. She tried a few more times but got no response. She took the master key and went to the room to see what the problem was. Before letting herself in, she knocked on the door but there was no answer. She unlocked the door and walked into the room. No one seemed to be around. She called out, "Is there anybody here?" There was still no response. She walked into the bathroom and saw a man on the commode slumped over. He seemed to be dead. As she moved closer, she knew with certainty that the man was dead because he was already turning blue. He had apparently been dead for several hours.

Polly felt sick to her stomach as she walked back to her office to call the police. He seemed like a really nice man when he'd rented the room the day before. It didn't take long for the police to arrive. An ambulance arrived shortly after the police. For the rest of the day, Polly couldn't stop thinking about the man. When she discovered him, his eyes had been wide open, and she couldn't erase the look on his face from her mind. The stench of death permeated the room. This was the craziest motel she had ever been sent to. From the day she arrived she had encountered problems that made her skin crawl. She had experienced an inexplicably uncomfortable feeling from the day she arrived at the airport. The day was gray and dreary, and the motel was located right next to the Interstate. The traffic noise was so loud that it interfered with sleep.

Polly never knew what to expect. Pensacola had been full of unpleasant surprises from the day she had arrived. Something was always happening on the Interstate. She looked forward to the day she could straighten out the mess at the motel, hire a new manager, and leave Florida for good. Even the climate disagreed with Polly. It was far too humid.

Ordinarily, Polly loved her job. She liked the excitement of not knowing where she would be sent or what she would encounter there. She also liked the aspect of her job that allowed her to meet new and interesting people. Pensacola, however, had proven to be a nightmarish experience. The rain poured down incessantly.

It took Polly weeks to get the motel operating at a respectable level. Her most difficult job was finding someone to run it. Most of the applicants were not qualified to run a motel of this magnitude. She interviewed several people for the job. One of the most important qualifications for the job was integrity. Most of the managers the company hired were honest, but unfortunately there had been some dishonest ones. The screening process was long and tedious. Polly spent a few more weeks getting everything in proper order.

The day Polly left Pensacola, she was extremely relieved. She flew back to El Paso, where Walt was waiting for her at the airport. Before they drove back to Las Cruces they went out to eat and share experiences they'd had during their separation. When they finally got home, they made love till they were both satisfied. Absence had made their hearts grow fonder, and they spent the next two days making love and enjoying each other's company. Polly took a few days off in order to get much needed rest. Pensacola had been a nightmare and she was exhausted. During her time off she cooked at home because she was tired of eating fast foods. She was hungry for home cooked roast beef, mashed potatoes with gravy, and green beans.

Walt was so happy to have her home that he spoiled her. She reveled in his attentions and pampering. Peggy, who also lived there, kept the house spotless and was becoming a very good cook. In Polly's absence, she took care of the motel and did an excellent job of it. Peggy was an asset to Polly. Polly had two daughters but they were both married and lived in Kansas. Her son Larry lived in Albuquerque, New Mexico. He had received his Master's degree and was working in a rest home as head administrator. Tommie, her youngest son, and his wife Jill also lived in Albuquerque. Tommie was a music promoter. It hadn't taken long for Tommie to acquire a few bands to manage. He had gotten them gigs all over the Southwest.

Polly loved the idea of having her sons close to her because it made it easier for them to visit her. Tommie had always wanted Polly and his dad to work things out. Polly explained to him that even though she still loved their father and would always love him, a reconciliation would never work because of his drinking. Tommie was really hurt over the divorce, and more than anything, wanted to be part of a family again. He missed all the fun they used to have together. He remembered the long Minnesota winters when the wind blew and it was too cold to go outside. They would sit in the family den and play cards. He wanted all that back, but it was never going to happen.

CHAPTER 28

Polly had inherited some money from her parents when they passed away. She decided to give each of her children a portion of her inheritance. Tommie, after receiving his share of the inheritance, decided he wanted to go back to Minneapolis, Minnesota and start his own business. He was very much like his mother. Once he set a goal he worked very hard at it. Not only was he a hard worker, he was also honest and fair. Even though Polly never voiced her feelings, she was very proud of her sons and their accomplishments, and she loved them very much. Destiny had separated her from her children but she had always been there for them.

Tommie went from town to town promoting the bands he managed, and he was very good at his craft. On one occasion, he was on the road promoting his hottest band, and road conditions were terrible. The fog was as thick as pea soup and visibility was almost nil. One of Tommie's associates was driving as they traveled a desolate road on their way from Brookings, South Dakota back to Minneapolis. Bill, who was driving, could barely see two feet in front of him when he suddenly collided with another car. A screech and the sound of shattering glass were the last sounds Tommie heard that foggy night. Tommie died on a desolate road in Minnesota.

Polly was in Las Cruces, New Mexico the night that Tommie died. She had no idea that he was in any kind of danger. Yet the night he died, Polly sensed that something was terribly wrong. Polly had spoken to Tommie on the phone early that same morning and had cautioned him to be careful before she said "goodbye". He had assured his mother that he would be all right, not realizing that his life was coming to an end. After the crash, Tommie lay dead after being thrown through the windshield and breaking his neck. Back in Las Cruces, Polly knew, as only a mother could know, that something terrible had happened to one of her children. The feeling was unshakable.

Within a couple of hours of Polly's chilling premonition, the phone rang. It was Jill, Tommie's wife. She was crying hysterically. Polly knew at that moment that something terrible had happened to Tommie. Jill told her that Tommie was dead. When Jill's words penetrated Polly's mind, she screamed, "No, Dear God, not my Tommie! Please, God, not my Tommie!" Her heart was shattered as the tears flowed. Walt tried to comfort her as she screamed, "My Tommie is dead!" Her mother's death had been a terrible blow, but it paled in comparison to the loss of her son. She was inconsolable.

Tommie was dead! Polly began going into shock as Walt brought her a glass of water, not knowing what else to do. She had spoken to Tommie just that morning. Everything had been fine. Now he was dead! The pain was unbearable for Polly, and she didn't know if she could survive a shattered heart. Her baby was dead, and there was no way she could bring him back!

She asked Peggy to call Larry, her oldest son, and break the news to him. Patti and Judie were also apprised of the devastating loss. Everyone was crying and trying to cope with the loss of their brother. It was a dark day for the Laffrenzen family.

When Tommie was small, he was a brat who gave his sisters a hard time. He was always making them cry, and they were always warning him that if he didn't stop they would tell Mom. Their threats didn't faze him. He was a natural born rascal who loved tormenting his sisters. His brother and sisters loved Tommie despite his childish pranks. To them, his death was incomprehensible. It didn't seem real.

In the morning, Polly drove from Las Cruces, New Mexico to Pipestone, Minnesota by herself. She was numb with grief. As the tears streamed down her face, a part of her found it difficult to accept that her Tommie was gone forever. As she traveled towards Minnesota, memories of Tommie as a child flooded her thoughts. Every once in a while reality hit her and her blood ran cold. She hadn't seen Tommie dead, so to preserve her sanity her mind only pictured him alive.

When she arrived in Amarillo, Texas, she couldn't drive any further. Polly drove to the airport, parked the car, and called Larry to tell him that she was going to fly from Amarillo to Sioux Falls, South Dakota. She asked him to take her car from the airport in Amarillo back to Pipestone.

Polly walked around the airport in Amarillo lost in thought. The people at the airport who saw Polly knew something was terribly wrong. Her face showed the pain that she carried in her heart. Her eyes were swollen from crying.

Sonny, Polly's brother, met her at Sioux Falls' airport. They hugged each other and started to cry. Polly and her brother had never been very close, but under these circumstances, their family bond evoked unexpected feelings of closeness. Polly had always felt good about returning to Pipestone, her hometown. This time, though, all she felt was pain and the dread of having to bury her son.

The day after Polly had arrived in Pipestone, Larry, Judie, Patti, and their father arrived in Pipestone. Everyone was feeling his own personal loss and tears flowed freely. Larry felt obligated to keep his father sober long enough to bury Tommie.

That evening, the family went to the funeral home to see Tommie. Actually seeing his lifeless body had a tremendously emotional impact on the entire family. Even though the family had been apart for quite some time, at this moment they needed each other. They could not go on with their lives until they let go of Tommie.

As they gathered together, they reminisced about what a character Tommie had been. They recalled his childhood antics and their own childhoods, of which Tommie was a part. Tommie's death made his family more aware of their own mortality.

Almost everyone in Pipestone attended Tommie's funeral. They wanted to bid farewell to one of their own. Tommie had been very popular in school and had even been a star basketball player. Because Pipestone was such a small community, everyone felt like family, and on this day they were forced to bid one of their sons "farewell". Pipestone was in mourning that day!

After the funeral, Tommie's family decided to drive to Sioux Falls, South Dakota and rent a room at a Super 8 Motel. They spent the night there before they drove back to New Mexico. Dale had moved to Las Cruces a few months earlier. He wanted to be near Polly because deep inside he was still madly in love with her. He was still a slave to the "bottle", and spent his days finding excuses to drink. He was an alcoholic who refused to admit his addiction or seek the help he desperately needed. He lived in a small apartment across town. Dale was almost 55 but looked much older. Alcohol had taken its toll on him. He had been a very handsome man but had sadly allowed alcohol to destroy not only his marriage, but his health and looks as well. All Dale had at this point in his life was the shirt on his back.

Dale had sold everything he and Polly had accumulated together during their marriage. He had sold the Calumet Hotel for $60,000 and had given most of the money to Judie, which had angered Patti, who wanted some of the money. Judie had been generous enough to share her good fortune with Patti and Larry. She loved them, and to her, family was more important than money.

In the days that followed, it was difficult for Polly to keep her mind on her job. To Polly, Tommie's death still seemed unreal. His death had devastated her and she found it difficult to find the strength to function. Now she truly understood the words "a broken heart" because she could hear the pieces of hers rattling in her chest. Only a mother who has lost a child could possibly begin to understand the pain Polly was feeling.

Walt offered Polly some comfort. He had always been there for her during the most difficult times of her life, and she cherished his friendship as well as his devotion to her.

Polly tried to put all her energy into her work in an effort to forget the excruciating pain she was enduring, but the memory of her precious Tommie relentlessly haunted her.

While Walt was at work, Polly would sit in her room and futilely wonder why God had taken her Tommie away from her. She thought, 'If only I had stayed in New Mexico, maybe he would still be alive.' The "if onlys" were driving her crazy. As much as she loved Las Cruces, she felt she needed to get away. Maybe it would do her some good to get involved in opening another motel in some distant place. Maybe then the horrendous pain might go away.

A few days had gone by when she got a call from the home office. Her bosses offered their condolences for her son's death and asked how she was feeling. She told them she was going through the most difficult time of her life. They asked her if she was ready to open another motel. Polly told them she was more than ready to get back to work. Work might take her mind off her pain.

Her other children called to see how she was doing. Polly felt very close to them right now and needed their emotional support. For the last few years, she had been so engrossed in her work that she hadn't had much time for them. She had many regrets, which caused a deep depression to envelop her. She asked herself the question, "What would I do differently if I had the chance to start over again?" The answer eluded her. Life seemed so unfair. Granted, God had been very good to her in many ways, and when her son died she didn't blame Him or anyone else. Nevertheless, the senselessness of his death at such a young age haunted her. She felt as if she had a heavy yoke chained around her neck. She knew her life would never be the same.

Two weeks after her son's death, Polly was sent to Ratón, New Mexico to open a new Super 8 Motel. Ratón was a quaint little town in northeastern New Mexico just south of Denver, Colorado on Interstate 25, and there wasn't much to do when darkness fell. The people in Ratón proved to be friendly and cooperative in doing business with the Motel 8 Corporation. They were very receptive to having a new motel built in their town. It would create new jobs and enhance their rural community. Ratón needed modernization.

Negative thoughts continued to consume Polly and left her feeling confused about a lot of things. She was now fifty-five years old. She resolved to give her total concentration to the work that lay ahead in an effort to quiet her agonizing thoughts and make the pain subside. On occasion, Polly would eat at a local diner, where she met some of the locals. They seemed very nice. Being so far away from home by herself seemed to be good therapy for her, even though she continued grieving for the son she had lost.

After a few weeks, the pain subsided somewhat, and she was thankful for her work. It helped keep her mind off her personal feelings.

When Polly left Ratón, she was sent to Farmington, New Mexico to redo the Super 8 Motel there. Because of her past experiences, going to Farmington was the last thing she wanted, but Ron Rivot told her not to worry about it, just to do it. As always, she did her job without complaint. She was very dedicated and good at what she did. Farmington was the same as it had been the last time she had been there. Polly really hadn't expected it to change overnight.

As was her habit, after working a long, hard day, Polly would draw a hot bath and soak for a long time. It was her way of relaxing. Afterward, if she felt up to it, she would go to the bar to drink a beer and play some pool with the local construction workers. Remembering all the things that had gone wrong the last time she'd been in Farmington left her feeling apprehensive. However, she had to put it behind her and do her best.

When she had completed the hiring of the staff, filling all the positions necessary for the motel to be in proper operation, Polly could leave and move onto her next project, wherever it might be. The nature of her job was never knowing where she would be sent once her immediate project was completed.

After being in Farmington for a month, she returned to Las Cruces. She missed Walt and her home very much. On her way home she anticipated Walt's lovemaking. She knew it would help relieve some of the pent-up pressure that had been building in both of them during their separation from each other. She felt a desperate need to have Walt make love to her and profess his love for her. She knew it would make her feel better about her life.

Walt asked Polly to quit her job with the company so he could take care of her for the rest of their lives. She couldn't do it. She loved her job too much. Walt was disappointed with her response and actually jealous of her work. He wanted Polly by his side all the time, not just occasionally. Little by little Polly and Walt began drifting apart. They each had different goals. Polly wanted to see the world while Walt just wanted to get married, settle down, and live happily ever after. It was sheer fantasy on his part. Of course, it never hurts to dream. He tried time and again to convince Polly to quit her job, but time and again she refused. He was frustrated and hurt by her stubbornness, and decided their relationship just wasn't going to work. One day he informed Polly that he was moving back to Pierre, South Dakota, and this time he would not be back. She told him that if that's what he wanted, maybe it would be best for both of them. One thing was for certain: Polly never wanted to marry again.

The following day, Walt was gone and Polly knew he would never return. Walt had been wonderful to her. He was honest and hard working. Polly had no complaints about him. His only flaw was his desire to get married. After Walt left Polly started drinking a lot, and after awhile, beer wasn't enough. She started drinking hard liquor. Vodka became her liquor of choice. Polly was in a lot of pain and tried to drown it by drinking. Her will to live was ebbing. She began downing a bottle of vodka every day and going to bars where she could meet men.

Walt's leaving had proved far more painful than Polly had anticipated. She never showed it, but deep inside she was desperately hurting, and the only way she could drown the hurt was to drink. Her son's death was also still eating away at her. Just when her career was peaking and she was reveling in her success, she had gotten knocked on her ass, and there seemed to be nothing she could do about it. She continued to drink in an effort to ease the pain, but it was futile.

Peggy would tell her she was drinking too much and that she'd better stop before she ended up killing herself. In a drunken slur, she would tell Peggy she didn't care because nothing mattered anymore.

Peggy tried convincing Polly to think of her remaining children, but to no avail. Polly just kept on drinking. Her constant drinking had begun to make her sick. Peggy was worried about Polly because she had quit eating, was losing a lot of weight, and was looking very frail and weak. When she spoke, Polly didn't make any sense. She had become seriously ill and was in desperate need of medical help. Peggy told her, "If you don't go and see a doctor, you're going to die." A little voice inside Polly's head warned her that she'd better look for some kind of help.

When Polly hit rock bottom and became scared enough, she got up from her bed barely able to move. She had aged immensely and was no longer the vivacious woman she had once been. Her will to live had shriveled, but by the grace of God, it hadn't died. That little voice inside her head kept nagging her to get help because her mission on this earth was as yet incomplete.

Peggy drove Polly to the doctor. The results of her physical examination were alarming. The doctor told Polly that she had to quit drinking or it would kill her. He also told her she was on the verge of a nervous breakdown. The doctor said she needed six weeks of bed rest, and that she had to start a healthy diet that included lots of fluids because her body was dangerously dehydrated. He also prescribed some sedatives to keep her calm.

When Polly got home, she went straight to bed and fell asleep. She experienced horrifying nightmares and woke up screaming. Peggy would run into the room to see if Polly was all right, and find her wide-eyed and sweating profusely. Polly had always been strong enough to deal with life's adversities, but the culmination of the tragedies that had beset her had finally taken their toll. She now had two choices –

follow the doctor's advice or die. This was the toughest test Polly had yet faced because she was used to being on the move all the time and she loved her work. With resignation, she closed her eyes and slept, praying she could survive this living nightmare. She asked God for the strength to survive. Polly had been through some really tough times lately.

Day after day she lay in bed trying to recuperate from the emotional turmoil and abuse that had taxed her poor body. It would be a steep climb but she had made the choice to live. Peggy fed her, making sure she had all the nutrition she needed to regain her strength. Within a few days, Polly began to be her normal self again. The first thing she wanted to know was how everything was going at her motel. Peggy assured her that everything was fine and she had nothing to worry about.

The stress and strain had taken their toll on Polly, but now she was on the road to recovery. Her skin color was returning, and her spirits were much lighter than they had been in quite awhile. Rest and the proper nutrition had done wonders for Polly. When she was feeling a little better, Polly tried to get out of bed. Peggy cautioned her that the doctor had prescribed complete bed rest for six weeks, and that she was going to see to it that Polly complied with the doctor's orders. Polly had come really close to killing herself by her heavy drinking. She was in so much pain that she didn't care if she lived or died, but Peggy wasn't going to let anything happen to her best friend. She took charge of Polly's recuperation.

After six weeks of convalescing, Polly's state of mind improved. She started working at the office. Her bosses from corporate headquarters called to see how she was doing. They wanted to know if she was ready to resume where she had left off. Polly told them she was quite ready.

God had always been so good to Polly, and at times she wondered why. Right now she needed to focus on the things that were important. Somehow she needed to get close to God. Polly had always had a healthy attitude about life and had always tried to be good to others. Granted, she had made some horrendous mistakes in her life. After all, no one is perfect, and life is a learning process. Polly's children called her daily to find out how she was doing. Since Larry and his wife were now living in Albuquerque, New Mexico, he made it a point to call her every day.

CHAPTER 29

After her recuperation, Polly was sent to the Super 8 Motel in Hobbs, New Mexico to straighten out the books that the last manager had messed up. It would take a miracle to get them in good order, but once again, Polly came to the rescue. Her uncanny ability to handle the most difficult situations is what made Polly so invaluable to her employers. She was without a doubt among the best in the business. Ron and Dennis, her bosses, counted on her expertise to mend whatever needed mending. Polly's integrity and reliability were her greatest strengths.

In 1987, Ron and Dennis decided to sell forty-five of their motels to Motels of America. Motels of America needed someone with Polly's knowledge, experience, and dedication. They offered her a position in their organization, but Polly refused. Polly told them that she wanted to stay in Las Cruces at the Super 8 Motel. Despite their efforts to convince her otherwise, Polly adamantly refused, and continued her employment with the Super 8 Motel Corporation.

The Super 8 Motel Corporation wanted Polly to go back east to run some of the motels that were having problems. Polly didn't want to go by herself so she invited Peggy along to help her. Peggy said she would be glad to accompany her. She had never been east before. The women caught a flight out of El Paso, Texas and flew to Dallas, Texas where they were bumped off their flight to Washington, D.C. They had to fly to Newark, New Jersey to pick up a company car. While they were waiting for their flight to New Jersey, Polly and Peggy decided to have a few cocktails. They had to wait so long at the airport that they ended up getting quite drunk.

Despite the wait, Polly and Peggy were having a great time. They always had such a good time whenever they were together that they took no notice of the people around them. They finally boarded their flight to Newark and continued their party on the plane. By the time they arrived at their destination they were feeling no pain.

When they picked up the rental car, they were so drunk that they didn't know where the hell they were or how they were going to get to Washington, D. C. It was one o'clock in the morning by the time they got on the freeway. Fortunately, they were headed in the right direction. Never had they encountered so much traffic. They drove all night, and thought they would never get there. The cars on the freeway moved really fast. The darkness, the coolness of the night, and the lines on the road seemed to create a rhythm. By the time they arrived in Washington, D. C., it was five o'clock in the morning. Both women were totally exhausted.

They drove to a dangerous part of town for two white females: an African-American neighborhood. A black police officer stopped them and asked, "What the hell are you doing in this part of town at this hour?" Polly explained to the officer that they were trying to find the Super 8 Motel. He told them he didn't know where it was, and that they'd better get back to their own side of town.

Polly and Peggy drove in an easterly direction in search of the Super 8 Motel. They stopped at an all-night convenience store where some black gentlemen in front of the store were eating chicken. Polly pulled up close to them, rolled down the car window, and asked if they knew where the Super 8 Motel was located. One of the men said, "Sure. I know where it's at. We installed the televisions there just yesterday." He gave the women directions on how to get to the motel while a couple of the other guys were giving Polly and Peggy the "evil eye". After they got directions, they drove out of there as fast as they could. The experience had completely sobered them up.

As they drove down the dark streets of Washington, D. C., they wished they could be back in Las Cruces, New Mexico. It was winter and very cold in Washington, while in Las Cruces the weather was warm all year round. Once in a while there'd be a cold spell, but not very often.

By the time they found the motel, it was almost six o'clock in the morning and they were so tired that all they wanted to do was get some sleep. Unfortunately, sleep would have to wait because they had a motel to open at 7:30 a.m. They had an hour-and-a-half to get ready. They regretted getting so drunk on their trip to D.C. because they were both painfully hung over and looked like hell, like they had been hit by a Mack truck. Peggy and Polly got the key to a room from the night auditor so they could put their things away and get cleaned up. At 7:00 a.m.

they were in the office and ready to work. Motel guests entered the office to check out. Peggy and Polly were so out of it, they didn't know what was going on.

Everything was in chaos. The books were a mess, but there was no time to straighten them out as there were more pressing matters to take care of. Some of the employees were calling to say they wouldn't be reporting for work. The place was a virtual nightmare.

Most of the staff consisted of African-Americans. They didn't seem to like Polly or Peggy. Polly tried to tell them what rooms she wanted cleaned but they ignored her. She knew right off that she wasn't going to like this place. Some of the ladies were so used to doing things their way that they weren't going to allow a white woman to change their routine. They were unruly, mean, and unfriendly, and even though most of the staff were hard workers, they didn't take directions well. Washington, D. C. was not what Polly thought it would be.

On their first Sunday off, Polly and Peggy decided to see the sights. They visited all the monuments and walked around the mall. Washington was a beautiful place, and there was a lot to see. The City Fathers had done a good job in laying out the design of this magnificent city. It was a marvel to behold! The city itself was just as unique as Polly imagined. The girls dined at some of the finest restaurants they had ever seen. The cuisine was superb.

Even in winter, people from all over America visited the capitol of the United States. Laughter filled the air as people from all walks of life inundated the city. After spending the day looking at everything they could, Polly and Peggy stopped at a local bar to have a drink and play some pool. To their dismay, it was time to return to the motel.

It took Polly and Peggy a month to straighten everything out. The company sent Peggy to Lexington to open a new motel while Polly remained in Washington to work by herself. She did not like it one bit! She had the habit of leaving the door to her motel unlocked. Some of the staff warned her not to leave the door unlocked because the area where the motel was located was not very safe. In Las Cruces the doors were left open all the time because there was nothing to fear, but this was not the case in the nation's capitol.

The company wanted Polly to take over this motel. The Super 8 Motel Corporation even offered Polly an increase in pay, but Polly said no. She had had her fill of this place, and she told them she was going back to Las Cruces. Washington, D.C. was the last place in the world she wanted to live. She told her new bosses that they'd better find a new manager for her to train. She was dead serious!

Polly called Peggy in Lexington and informed her of her intention to return to Las Cruces. She told Peggy, "This big city is not my cup of tea." Polly also said that the attitude of some of the people didn't sit well with her. Peggy told her that she wasn't going to stay either. She didn't like the East Coast anymore than Polly did.

The Super 8 Motel Corporation wanted Polly to take over the entire motel chain on the East Coast. They even offered to move all her belongings to Washington. Polly was already getting on in years, and there was no way in hell that she was going to move. Besides, what if they decided to let her go? She'd be stuck. There was no way she was going to take that chance. She was adamant when she told the company they'd better find somebody else.

A week later, Polly and Peggy caught a flight back to Las Cruces, New Mexico. They had both had their fill of the East Coast. There was no place like home for either of them. Polly had been on the road for many years opening one motel after another all across the country. She was ready to settle down. Her new bosses kept calling her almost every day pleading with her to reconsider their offer. Time and again, Polly refused.

After a few weeks, Polly knew she had to do something to bring in some income. Peggy told Polly that she was going to Colorado to live with her sister. Around the same time, the Super 8 Motel Corporation called Polly and asked her if she would like to go to Dillon, Colorado and take over a franchise Super 8 Motel in big trouble and in need of someone to rescue it from bankruptcy. Polly told them she'd love to but, there were some matters she had to take care of first. That night, Polly and Peggy decided to go out on the town, have a few beers, and play pool, as well as visit some friends they hadn't seen in a while.

As they were playing pool, a very handsome man in his late forties walked in. He and Polly exchanged looks and smiled at each other. She felt a tingle run up her spine, and her heart started to pound. It had been a while since she'd been with a man. Tonight she was ready for love. The handsome devil made his way over to the table where Polly and Peggy were sitting. He took Polly's hand and said, "Hi. My name is Rick." Polly said in an effervescent voice, "Well, hi there Rick. My name is Paulyn but you can call me Polly." Peggy also introduced herself to Rick, who seemed a nice enough fellow. Polly was instantly attracted to him from the moment she laid eyes on him. He was very good-looking, clean cut, and smelled wonderful. The ladies asked Rick to sit with them and have a drink. He gladly accepted their offer, and sat next to Polly. He ordered a beer, and before long, they were all having a good time.

Polly and Rick went out on the dance floor and slow danced. It had been awhile, but Polly was still a great dancer. Rick complemented her on how good a dancer she was, whereby she replied, "Thanks. You're quite a good dancer yourself." As they danced cheek to cheek, Polly reveled in the feel of Rick's firm body. It felt good being in his arms. Their breathing was becoming irregular as they moved around the dance floor. She sensed Rick was becoming aroused. Polly needed affirmation that she was still desirable. That night, she and Rick ended up making love. Polly really liked Rick, and they became inseparable.

As the day for her departure to Dillon, Colorado, approached, Polly asked Rick if he would like to go with her. He said he would as he had nothing better to do. That night, Polly packed up all her things, and in the morning she and Rick were up at the crack of dawn. It took most of the day to drive to Dillon.

When they arrived at the Super 8 Motel, Polly went into the office to talk to the night auditor and obtain the key to one of the motel rooms.

Rick and Polly were getting along splendidly. He was forty-eight years old and Polly was now fifty-eight. They seemed to be able to talk comfortably about anything and everything. After cleaning up, they went out to get something to eat at a small local tavern. Most of the townsfolk were very nice. Dillon was nestled in a valley surrounded by mountains, which were still covered with snow and presented a spectacular sight. It was a veritable paradise. Even the air seemed fresher and pollution-free. It was amazing how green everything was. Polly loved it!

Dillon, Colorado had definitely captured Polly's heart. She had hated all the commotion and pollution on the East Coast. By comparison, Dillon was a tranquil paradise. Rick had come into her life at just the right time. Polly needed someone she could talk to who would listen to her problems and help her keep everything in proper perspective.

The following morning, she met with the owners of the Super 8 Motel to discuss why they were so close to bankruptcy. In the course of their discussion, Polly discovered that bad bookkeeping was the major culprit. She told the owners that it would take her a while to straighten everything out. Polly advised them that she needed full control of the motel in order to salvage it. The owners agreed to her terms and Polly went to work on the books, which were in complete disarray.

The motel was run incompetently. Most of the rooms were rented almost every day, but the owners were squandering the money and neglecting to pay the bills. Polly worked her fingers to the bone on the first day and hadn't made a dent on the enormous amount of paperwork. It was a grind getting the messy bookkeeping in order. She plugged away at it every day. At the end of the day, Polly and Rick would go out to dinner at different restaurants.

On her first Sunday off, Polly and Rick drove up to Vail, Colorado to see what all the talk was about. She had heard a lot about what a great place Vail was. When they arrived in Vail, she saw for herself that it was every bit as beautiful as she had heard it was.

Vail was a skier's paradise inhabited by wealthy skiers during the winter months. The rich lived in condos at the base of the mountain. Fancy cars could be seen parked by the condos. Many of the people around the village looked as if they came from affluent families. Most were Easterners. During the peak of the ski season, there were literally hundreds of people on the slopes.

When Polly and Rick visited Aspen, Colorado, they discovered that it was quite similar to Vail in attracting the very rich. After their arrival in Aspen, they rented a room, cleaned up, and went dancing. Most of the people she and Rick saw were quite young. A youthful buoyancy seemed to fill the air as young couples walked hand in hand. The distinct aroma of marijuana was overpowering. Aspen was apparently a party town for the wealthy. White Americans were in the majority.

Aspen proved to be a very expensive town. A hamburger cost $7.00 and a motel room cost no less than $100.00 a night. One night in Aspen was all Polly and Rick could afford, but it was an unforgettable night. The beer pubs were filled with customers from all walks of life getting liquored up. It was also obvious that there was an abundance of drugs because everyone seemed to be higher than a kite. The wealthy had made the little town of Aspen their own little paradise. Aside from all the partying, though, there were serious as well as famous skiers who came from all over the world to ski the infamous devil runs on Aspen Mountain.

That night, Polly and Rick mingled with the crowds and joined in the fun. They got quite drunk before returning to their motel room, where they made love and fell asleep in each other's arms. In the morning they drove back to Dillon.

It took Polly almost a month to get the books in order. Even after the books had been straightened out, the Super 8 Motel was still far from being financially stable. Polly had worked very hard to straighten out the mess that had confronted her when she arrived, but the motel owners had to do their part if they wanted it to survive. One of the first things they had to do was stop living beyond their means. If they cooperated, the owners would be able to see the light at the end of the tunnel in just a couple of months.

Polly was having second thoughts about working for the Super 8 Motel Corporation. It was her dream to own a motel. The company wanted her to go back, either to Washington, D. C. or to one of the other motels on the East Coast. She had had her fill of the East Coast and told the company she wanted to stay in Las Cruces. She was too old to be moving again, knowing that if the company decided to let her go, she would be stranded with all her belongings in a city she hated.

During their stay in Dillon, Rick and Polly visited a different part of Colorado every weekend. They wanted to see all the small towns nestled in the high mountains. Driving through the mountains was a real rush. She and Rick would find a campground where they could relax by a peaceful stream. They would also take short hikes through the many small trails. Polly and Rick spent as much time as they could in the mountains enjoying the fresh air and solitude.

When her job was completed at the Super 8 Motel in Dillon, Polly was sent to Farmington, New Mexico to work out some problems with one of the Super 8 Motels. She knew this would be her last job for the Super 8 Motel Corporation.

The more she thought about it, the more convinced she was that she would purchase a motel of her own no matter what it took so that she could remain in Las Cruces. Polly wanted to spend the rest of her life in Las Cruces, since she had come to consider it her home.

While Polly was working hard in an effort to get her new project back on track, Rick was spending his time at the bars getting drunk. It was a real turn-off for Polly. He had become too much like her husband Dale. She had no doubt that at some point she would dump him. Memories of her life with Dale flashed in her mind and she was damned if she would live that way again. Rick had turned out to be not only a drunk, but a gigolo as well. He obviously had no worthwhile goals and absolutely no ambition.

One day while Polly was hard at work, Rick was involved in an automobile accident that left her car totaled. He was lucky he came out alive. It was the only car she owned. He was so much like Dale, Polly knew she had made a big mistake by getting involved with him. It was definitely time to get rid of him, but she wasn't sure how. Their sexual relationship was great, but she knew there was more to life than sex. There was no way she was going to put up with another Dale.

Polly was so infuriated with Rick for wrecking her car that she told him she didn't want him around any more. To her dismay, the guy just wouldn't go away. He told her how sorry he was and that he would replace the car. She had been down this road before. Polly had believed Dale's temporary remorse and empty promises because she loved him, but there was no way she was going to make the same mistake with Rick. She told Rick she wanted him out of her house. Evidently he didn't take her seriously, and made no attempt to leave. In retrospect, Polly knew she had made a big mistake when she became involved with Rick. He was always broke, and although he got odd jobs, he never had a steady job.

From the day they met that fateful night at the bar, Peggy hadn't liked Rick. She had cautioned Polly not to get involved with him because she had a strong feeling that he spelled trouble. Peggy was right! Rick was a leech that Polly couldn't seem to get rid of.

Polly didn't want to work for the Super 8 Motel Corporation any more, so she resigned her position with the company. She wanted to find a job closer to home. She had a lot of friends in the motel business, and one day, a friend told her that there was a motel for sale. The owner of the motel that was up for sale was Bob Lilly, star football player of the Dallas Cowboys.

Polly had a part-time job at the RV Park next door, so she walked over to the office and asked the auditor if he had heard the rumor that Bob Lilly had a motel for sale. The auditor told her it wasn't a rumor – the motel was for sale. Polly asked if he knew the asking price. The auditor told her it was in the area of $600,000. Having been in the motel business for so many years, Polly knew it was a steal at that price. Now all she had to figure out was how to get her hands on that kind of money. She knew a bank loan would be next to impossible because she was a woman. Polly was determined to find the financing because she really wanted this motel. It needed a little work, but with a little TLC, she had no doubt she could get it back in shape. She had done it before when she bought the Calumet Hotel. After she purchased the Calumet, she had worked long and hard to get it operational, and she knew she could do the same with the motel Bob Lilly was selling.

Polly was a woman with a dream, and she was determined to make it come true. She contacted Bob Lilly and told him that she was interested in buying the motel. It so happened that the RV Park and the restaurant next to Bob Lilly's motel were also on the market. Polly's mind was racing. She had great credit and money in one of the banks in Las Cruces where she had been banking for several years, and she was acquainted with all the employees.

Having worked in the banking business when she was very young, she knew how they worked. Polly informed the main loan officer of her plans. He made Polly fill out a financial statement. After it was completed, the loan officer went over it and asked her a few questions. He then told her that he would have to discuss it with the Board before deciding if she qualified for a loan. Polly wanted to borrow a large amount of money, and getting Board approval didn't look very promising. The loan officer told Polly he would have an answer for her by the following day.

In her heart, Polly knew that purchasing the motel was the best thing that could happen, not only for her, but for Peggy as well. She was tired of being on the road. She was ready for the stability she had never had because of her career. If by some miracle the deal went through, her life as well as Peggy's would change. They would have a lot of work ahead of them but it would be worth it. That night, she and Peggy went out to eat at a local bar where they also played some pool with a few friends. During the entire evening Polly kept wondering if the bank would lend her the money. Her chances of getting a bank loan were slim to none but she refused to give up hope.

The next day, the bank called her and requested that she stop by the bank so they could discuss some things with her. She told them that she would be right over. Polly wanted to make a good impression, so she chose her attire carefully and made sure her demeanor exuded confidence. When she arrived at the bank, Polly felt extremely nervous. She had always worked for somebody else. Now she would be her own boss.

As she entered the office of the loan officer, she felt a calm confidence wash over her. The commercial officer was waiting for her. He was in his mid-fifties and quite handsome. He had dark brown hair, a thin mustache, and wore glasses. He had been with the bank since its inception and had worked his way up to commercial officer. Polly sat in a chair directly in front of his desk. He looked at her for a moment and then said, "Congratulations, Mrs. Laffrenzen. The Board has approved your request for a loan to buy the Coach Light Inn Motel, the RV Park, and the restaurant." Polly was speechless! It took a while for the information to sink in. She regained her composure and said, "Thank you. You won't regret it." She signed all the documents necessary to finalize the transaction. Her dream was finally coming true. Evidently the bank believed in her venture as well as in her ability to succeed. The fact that she had been a good customer for many years worked in her favor.

Polly couldn't believe she had pulled it off. She now had the financial backing to fulfill her dream. As she walked out of the bank, her feet barely touched the ground. She felt totally exhilarated. Polly hadn't been this happy in a very long time. She no longer had to go from town to town never knowing what she would encounter. Her only concern now was to make a success of her own motel. She had been on the road for over ten years traveling to every corner of America. As much as she had loved her job, she

hated the loneliness of going from one town to another and being surrounded by strangers.

CHAPTER 30

The day arrived when Bob Lilly handed over the keys to the motel and she handed him a cashier's check for $600,000. Words can't describe the happiness she felt on that most auspicious occasion. This hundred-room motel on Motel Boulevard in Las Cruces, New Mexico now belonged to her! It was a dream come true.

The motel was in dire need of some serious repairs. As Polly, Peggy and Rick surveyed each room, they made a punch list. Every room was painted a weird color and nothing matched. The plates on all the light receptacles had been painted over. The curtains were very old and in need of laundering. The stench in the rooms was unbelievable. There wasn't one room that didn't need some form of repair.

For the first time since Polly and Rick had been living together, he volunteered to help her renovate the motel. Peggy was just as excited as Polly about the whole thing. She could finally have the security she had always wanted. It took them almost all day to complete the punch list. The first thing they had to do was get the locks changed. Rick offered to do it. Polly was shocked at his willingness to help. Maybe there was hope for this guy after all.

While Peggy began cleaning one room at a time, Polly and Rick went to the local hardware store to buy new locks. Repairing the motel was going to be very expensive. The former owners had let it deteriorate, and it was going to take a lot of money to undo the damage.

When they returned to the motel, Rick began the task of changing all the locks while Polly and Peggy began doing the laundry. The sheets and pillowcases were so filthy they no longer looked white. Apparently they had never been rinsed properly because the washing machine was so full of soap residue that it overflowed onto the floor. The Mexican lady who worked for the motel washed the laundry but never bothered to rinse it.

Rick worked diligently for a couple days without stopping. Evidently Rick had seen the light and realized that Polly needed help. At the end of the day, Polly bought a case of beer and they sat around drinking beer and relaxing. They talked about all the work that lay ahead, acknowledging it was worth it. They ended up renting as many rooms as they could.

It was November 5, 1987. It was cold and snowing. It snowed in Las Cruces very seldom, but on this particular day there was a massive snowfall. The Interstate had to be closed. Many people were stranded in Las Cruces. There weren't enough rooms at the motel to accommodate such a large influx of people. Polly decided to open up all the rooms that were habitable.

People were everywhere. Some of them were even sleeping on the floor. It was freezing that night, and travelers entered the motel in droves hoping to find shelter. The children were the ones that worried Polly. It made her very happy to be able to offer some form of shelter to anyone who needed it. The motel looked like a homeless shelter with people sprawled all over the place.

Polly had a lot of things to take care of, such as buying liability insurance, interviewing prospective employees, and staffing the motel. She needed cleaning ladies as well as maintenance men. She had done this for her former employers and now, to her great joy, she was doing it for herself.

That night, as she and Rick lay in bed, they talked about all the work that lay ahead of them. Rick assured her he would help her in whatever way he could. This made Polly very happy. Not long ago she was ready to throw him out, and now here they were making love. Life was unpredictable and wonderful! Rick genuinely loved Polly. There were so many things about her that made him happy. He had come to realize that he didn't want to lose her.

At the crack of dawn, Polly looked out of the window, and the sight of the snow-blanketed earth took her breath away. People were trying to start their cars so they could get back on the road again. Polly took a quick shower and went down to the office. No sooner had she unlocked the office door when people wanting to check out surrounded her. Everyone was thanking her for her efforts to accommodate them. Polly told them she could have done no less. Sheltering the stranded travelers was Polly's way of thanking God for his generosity towards her.

All morning people kept coming in to check out and thank her for her hospitality on such a ruthless night. Polly felt really good about being able to help so many people. She was overwhelmed by their gratitude.

In the meantime, Rick went to the restaurant next door and got breakfast for both of them. As Polly and Rick were eating breakfast, Peggy walked in and said she wasn't feeling very well. She thought she might have the flu. Polly told her to go to her room and lay down, but Peggy said there was too much work to do since they only had a skeleton crew. Polly told Peggy to stay and take care of the office while she went to the dreaded laundry room they had named "Fiasco". No sooner had Polly put in the sheets to wash when mountains of bubbles started to overflow from the machine. The laundry room filled with bubbles. It was a nightmare. After each load of sheets was washed and dried, Polly would take them to the office so Peggy could fold them. Rick, in the meantime, was busy painting the rooms and getting them ready for renting.

Day after day they worked vigorously trying to get the motel in decent shape. There were one hundred rooms, and Polly wanted to rent all of them if she could. She started renting rooms to some of the local riffraff by the month. She had a $10,000-a-month mortgage payment and needed to rent as many rooms as she possibly could. In order to make the mortgage payment, Polly had no choice but to rent to anyone in need of a room, even the dregs of the community, as long as they could pay.

This particular winter was colder than any she had experienced in many years. It was November, and it was so cold that no one wanted to be without a place to stay. The Coach Light Inn, Polly's motel, accommodated not only the poor and deprived, but also drug addicts and derelicts. Polly turned some of the rooms into business offices, which she rented by the month. Peggy, Polly, and Rick were working long, exhausting hours every single day, but Polly was determined to make it in the motel business. "Failure" was not part of her vocabulary. Every day they had one more room ready to rent. The going was slow but steady. There were so many repairs to be made that Polly was constantly dishing out money. At night when Polly finally went to bed, she was totally exhausted and fell into a deep sleep.

Making the insurance payment every month wasn't easy. Polly had bought insurance from a friend they had met at a local bar. Every month, like clockwork, the insurance agent would show up to pick up the premium. Peggy would comment that he was there to rip them off again.

Because of the condition of the sheets, they never had to buy soap because the sheets were so saturated with it from lack of rinsing by the previous owner's staff.

Polly felt good about the progress they were making. Unfortunately, Polly and Rick's relationship wasn't faring so well. It was on the decline. They were arguing more and more, and Rick was becoming far too possessive. Polly and Peggy liked going bowling with some of their girl friends. After one of their girls' nights out, they got home rather late. Rick was really pissed. He asked Polly, "Where the hell have you been?" Polly was half-looped and feeling no pain. Her flippant attitude added fuel to Rick's already escalating rage and he slapped her across the face, knocking her to the floor. Polly began to cry and angrily asked Rick, "Why the hell did you do that, you asshole?" He slapped her again. She picked herself up off the floor, went into the bedroom, and locked the door.

As Polly lay on the bed crying, she wondered about her choices in men. She was a free-spirited person who unwittingly chose domineering men. Her kind-heartedness and understanding nature must have been interpreted as weakness because the men in her life always seemed to take advantage of her. The way she felt at this moment, they could all go to hell! She was determined to get that gigolo son-of-a-bitch out of her life once and for all. The fact that he had worked hard with the restoration of the motel didn't give him the right to abuse her, and she would never forgive him for hitting her.

No matter what Polly said, Rick wouldn't leave. Polly and Peggy had grown to dislike Rick, and they both let him know it every chance they got. Instead, he became more possessive with Polly, and when he drank he became more violent. Polly was terrified of him and didn't want to be alone with him anymore.

One night, he and Polly got into a vicious argument over his jealousy. It escalated to the point where Polly actually had to call the police. To her dismay, the police told her there was nothing they could do unless he actually attempted to kill someone. Polly was enraged by their lack of solicitude for her safety.

Having decided that she couldn't live in daily fear for her life, Polly told Rick that she wanted him out of her motel and out of her life for good. Rick went ballistic. He grabbed a knife and threatened to kill her. She knew he meant it and took off running. Polly managed to call the police, and she and Peggy hid in one of the rooms until they arrived. When the police finally arrived, Rick got into a big argument with them. It took six officers to handcuff him as he was a very strong man. He was jailed for, among other things, assaulting a police officer. After a few days in jail, he was released.

After his release, Rick went back to the motel begging Polly to forgive him and promising he would never do it again. He bought her flowers and told her how very much he loved her, vowing he would never hurt her again. Gullible Polly believed him.

Rick's contrition didn't last very long. No sooner had he conned Polly into letting him stay than he knocked her around again. Polly called the police again. This time Polly placed a Restraining Order on him. According to the Restraining Order, he was to stay 100 feet away from Polly. Rick began stalking her and wouldn't leave her alone. It terrified Polly not knowing what Rick might do. She called the police to tell them that he had violated the Restraining Order. The police would throw him in jail, but, once he was released, he would resume his stalking. Nothing Polly said seemed to get through to Rick. She decided to overcome her fear as best she could and get on with her life hoping and praying that Rick would fade away.

Little by little, the motel began looking pretty good. Most of the rooms were now rented. She hired her own crew of cleaning ladies, a maintenance man, and a new housekeeper. Many of the tenants rented by the month, and most of them were really good about paying their rent on time. There were those few who were always late with their rent payments. Many of her tenants were drifters and low-lifes, but Polly didn't have the heart to turn anyone away.

CHAPTER 31

In January, two months after Polly opened the Coach Light Inn, her ex-husband Dale Laffrenzen died in his apartment across town. He had moved from Minnesota to be close to Polly. Despite the drinking that had destroyed their marriage, Polly still loved Dale. They had remained good friends until the day he died. She was going through a really rough period in her life, mostly because of Rick. He was still stalking her and harassing her on the telephone. Dale's death was just one more cross to bear. Even though they had been divorced for many years, his death hit her hard. In their twenty-five years of marriage they had shared many good times together. Dale had been an extremely handsome man with a very outgoing personality.

Their daughters Patti and Judie had moved to Las Cruces so that they could be near their mother. Both of them had left their husbands. Dale loved his children very much, and Tommie's death had devastated him. He had never completely recovered from his son's untimely death. After Polly and Dale divorced,

Tommie had stayed with his father to help him run the Calumet Hotel. Tommie and Dale had been very close, and after Tommie's death Dale's drinking got further out of control. Tommie had always been his favorite child. When he died Dale's will to live all but disappeared. The only thread that kept him connected to life was his great love for Polly. He hated the fact that he was a drunk but felt helpless in the throes of such a treacherous disease. Medically, Dale's death was the result of a heart attack. In reality, he had died of a broken heart.

Judie, the youngest daughter, took her father's death the hardest. Dale's children loved him dearly, and even though they were disappointed by his excessive drinking, they never treated him with disrespect. Even after the divorce, they had always hoped their parents would get back together. Now they were viewing their father's lifeless body at the funeral home.

In his will, Dale left everything to his daughter Judie. His daughter Patti was livid because he had left her nothing. She was so angry that she stormed out of the room in which the will was being read. Judie, however, was not a greedy person, and shared her inheritance with Larry and Patti. For her, this was a time for grieving, not for haggling over money.

Dale's younger brother Dave made the trip from California to pay his last respects. Dave and Polly had always gotten along quite well. Dale and Polly had started dating when Dave was twelve years old. He had a crush on Polly. One day when he was out selling papers, he stopped by Polly's apartment and just sat there staring at her. He finally worked up the courage to ask her if she would teach him how to kiss. She asked, "Aren't you a bit young for that?" Dave answered, "I'm almost thirteen, Polly. Please teach me how to kiss." Polly was reluctant but said, "Come here, little boy. I'll give you a lesson on how to kiss but you'd better not tell anybody." He smiled as he crossed his heart and said, "I promise I won't tell anyone." Dave sat next to Polly, who then gave him a kissing lesson. From that day forward, Dave would blush every time he was around Polly.

Dave had been living in California for many years, and like his older brother was a heavy drinker. He was just as handsome as Dale. Dave was tired of life in California and asked Polly if she needed someone to help her run the motel. Polly told him she could use help in the office. She was going through a really rough period, and Dave's arrival couldn't have been timed better. Rick was still harassing her. Having Dave around made her feel safer. He was an accountant and quite good at bookkeeping. Dave was not only a hard worker, he was also very honest. He and Polly got along really well.

Dave joined Polly and Peggy in getting the motel renovated so they could rent all of the rooms. It was a great relief when the job was finally completed. Polly was not one to leave a job unfinished no matter how much time or work it took. When they saw how good the motel looked, they felt great satisfaction.

Now that all the hard work was behind them, they could relax. Polly, Peggy, and Dave could go out to dinner, slam down a few beers and play pool. By the time they got home, the three of them were quite tipsy. Polly and Dave would stay up late playing cards and getting reacquainted. They had been apart for so many years that they had a lot of catching up to do. Because of all the turmoil in her life at that time, Polly welcomed Dave's friendship. She was scared to death of Rick since he had already tried to kill her, and Dave's presence gave her a sense of security.

As they reminisced, Dave told Polly that he had always been attracted to her. He asked if she would like to go to Mexico with him. She told him that it had been a long time since she had gone anywhere because she had been too busy working. She couldn't recall a time in the past ten years when she had taken a real vacation because the motel business required so much of her time. She was ready for one. The thought of basking on the beach was heavenly. Polly eagerly accepted Dave's invitation.

The following week, Polly and Dave flew to Cabo San Lucas. As the plane ascended to 30,000 feet, pictures of sandy beaches and colorful sunsets danced in Polly's head. As the plane carried them to their destination, Polly and Dave ordered drinks. Dave downed his drink as if it were water and ordered another. Polly took notice of how much Dave was drinking but decided not to become too concerned. After all, they were on vacation.

When they arrived in Cabo San Lucas, they took a cab to their hotel. The weather was fabulous. It was indeed a vacationer's paradise. There was an influx of people, especially young people. Polly was very much attracted by the tan, muscular bodies of the men she saw.

The hotel where they were staying had palm trees all along the entranceway. It had a delicious tropical atmosphere that elicited feelings of anticipation and excitement. There was a cobblestone driveway with sandstone planters. The portal was huge with intricately designed corbels and beautiful tin-printed chandeliers. There was a revolving door where bellmen waited to help with the luggage and usher the guests into the hotel. The lobby of the hotel was just as impressive as the portal through which Polly and Dave had entered. The ceilings were twenty feet high with beautifully carved *vigas*. The aroma of Mexican cuisine permeated the lobby. The smell of the food made Polly hungry. She was famished and ready for some delicious seafood.

After checking in and freshening up, Polly and Dave took the elevator back down to the lobby. Upon entering the dining room, they noticed that it was packed with American tourists having lunch. Conversation filled the air. Polly and Dave were seated at a table next to a window located near an outdoor patio with a large swimming pool. Young and old people were either swimming or just sunbathing and drinking exotic drinks served at the poolside bar. The drinks that Dave and Polly ordered looked Polynesian and tasted delicious. They also ordered a tray that contained a variety of seafood. Both ate until they were full and couldn't eat another bite.

Polly noticed that Dave looked a little under the weather, but since he hadn't complained that he wasn't feeling well, she didn't bring it to his attention. When they finished eating, they strolled hand in hand out to the poolside where people were talking and laughing. They walked across the patio to some stairs that led to the beach. The beach was just as inundated by tourists as the hotel. These people were either swimming, wading in the shallow water, or sunbathing. The aura of fun and escape made Polly glad she had decided to take a well-earned vacation, leaving her trusted friend Peggy to take care of business.

Dave and Polly had walked along the beach for about a mile when Dave turned to Polly and said, "I think we should go back. I'm not feeling very well."

Polly asked, "What's wrong?" He told her he was just feeling a bit lightheaded, but by the time they reached the hotel Dave's face was white as a sheet. Polly asked him if he needed a doctor, but he declined and said he'd be okay if he just rested for awhile. Polly lay next to him, and before too long they were asleep in each other's arms.

In the morning, Polly saw that Dave didn't look any better than he had the night before, and he evidently didn't feel any better. As a matter of fact, he was feeling much worse. This worried Polly. She told him she was going to call a doctor but he said, "Don't worry. I'll be all right." Polly asked if he would like something to eat but he said he wasn't hungry. Polly said she was hungry and was going to get something to eat. Their room was on the tenth floor, so she took the elevator down to the lobby, where a mass of people were either checking in or checking out. There were just as many crowding the lobby as there had been the day before. Polly walked into the dining room and noticed that it was packed with diners. The maitre d' escorted her to a table, and as she ordered steak and eggs for breakfast, she couldn't get Dave off her mind. She couldn't figure out how he could have gotten sick so suddenly. Polly speculated that maybe the drinking water had made him ill. When she was finished eating, she returned to their room to find Dave asleep. She decided to take a walk along the beach. She loved looking at the ocean. Polly spent the remainder of her vacation roaming the beach while Dave spent his sick in bed.

When they returned to Las Cruces, Polly took Dave to the doctor. After examining him, the doctor told Polly that Dave had cirrhosis of the liver and had maybe two months to live. Peggy and Polly were broken-hearted because they had grown very fond of

Dave. They did everything they could to make him as comfortable as possible.

The motel was doing really well but wouldn't start showing a profit for another five years or so. It had taken a lot of work and perseverance to revive it. Peggy and Polly had overcome a lot of obstacles in the process. Even though Dave was sick, he had been a godsend. Polly and Peggy had grown very fond of him. Dave had been a big help to them. His impending death was constantly on their minds. Dave knew he was dying and that if he didn't quit drinking completely, he would die a lot sooner than the doctor had predicted, but he just kept drinking.

Meanwhile, Rick was still calling Polly and harassing her. He pleaded with her to take him back, telling her how much he still loved her and how he couldn't live without her. His pleas fell on deaf ears. Polly told Rick, "I'm living with someone else. He's very good to me." Rick started crying and pleaded, "Please, Polly, give me another chance. I'll never hit you again." Polly replied, "You had your chance and you blew it, now get over it because I'm moving on with my life." The only time Rick called was when he was drunk or down. Polly had been good to him and had supported him during the duration of their relationship. When she ended the relationship, Polly promised herself she would never take care of another man as long as she lived.

Late one afternoon, Dave said he had to run an errand and would be back in about an hour. Polly said, "Okay, but be careful and don't take any wooden nickels." Dave said, "Okay." He kissed her and was gone. Polly kept thinking, 'I hope he hasn't been drinking too much.' He had a couple of bottles stashed in his room and would nip from them all day long. He knew he was dying because of his drinking but had evidently chosen to leave this world with a drink in his hand.

A couple of hours had passed and Dave hadn't returned. Polly was beginning to get really worried, hoping he wasn't at some bar getting drunk. The night auditor was working while Polly paced the floor waiting for Dave to get home. A few more hours passed and Dave still wasn't home. Polly grew more worried. Suddenly the phone rang. As she answered it, she prayed that it was Dave calling to tell her he would be home soon. To her shock, it was the Coroner's Office calling to ask if she could go in and identify a body. Her heart was in her throat because she instinctively knew it was Dave. She began to cry as she grabbed her coat and headed towards the Coroner's Office.

When Polly finally arrived at the hospital, she asked for directions to the State Coroner's Office. As she entered the office, she encountered a bald man in his mid-sixties smoking a cigar. Polly asked for "Mr. Jones". The pudgy little man said, "I'm Mr. Jones. May I help you?" Polly replied, "I'm Polly Laffrenzen. You called me a half hour ago and asked if I could identify a body." Mr. Jones said, "Follow me, please." They walked down a small corridor. At the end of the corridor was a door, which Mr. Jones opened. As the door opened, a blast of cold air hit them, sending shivers down Polly's spine. They entered the stair-well. As they descended the stairs, their footsteps echoed in the silence. After reaching the bottom of the stairs, they came to a dark, cold corridor. The dampness permeated the air. The place gave Polly the willies.

Not a word had been spoken by either Mr. Jones or Polly since the initial introduction. Polly kept wondering whose body awaited her. They reached a room with double doors and walked inside. It was a size-able room with tables where they apparently per-formed the autopsies. Lined along the wall were cabinet doors. Polly's heart was racing faster. Mr. Jones reached for the handle of a large cabinet door and pulled on it. Polly could hear her heart thumping. Mr. Jones pulled out the drawer. There was a body covered by a bloody sheet. Mr. Jones asked Polly to step closer. As she moved closer, Mr. Jones pulled back the sheet and Polly saw it was Dave. She screamed! Her stomach got queasy and she felt like puking. Her mind began to race as she wondered what had happened. There was blood everywhere. Polly asked, "What in the world happened?" The coroner replied, "A car struck him on the Interstate. He was killed instantly. Apparently his car had swerved off the road and down an embankment. He got out and walked right into oncoming traffic. The driver of the car that hit him tried to avoid him, but it was too late as he was already flying through the air. He died of trauma to the head. His blood alcohol level was .35. I don't think he even knew what hit him."

After the initial shock of seeing Dave dead and bloody had worn off a bit, tears streamed down Polly's face. Once again she was in mourning for someone she loved. The fact that Dave had been dying was little consolation for the horrible way he died. Polly was still grieving for Tommie and Dale. She couldn't help but wonder who would be next. "I take it you know this man?", the Coroner asked. "Yes, I do. He's my brother-in-law," Polly answered. Her heart was in such pain that she wanted to die. Having experienced the death of three people she loved in such a short span of time, she wondered how much pain her poor heart could bear. In her mind she reasoned, 'If I were dead I wouldn't have to feel this kind of excruciating pain.'

As she drove back to the motel, she couldn't remember ever feeling as depressed as she did at the present moment. The tears wouldn't stop. She felt like drowning her sorrows in the bottle, and as soon as she could, she would. The grief was overwhelming. This was one of the darkest moments in Polly's life.

When she got back to the motel, Polly broke the sad news to Peggy. Peggy was in a state of disbelief and asked Polly, "What did you say?" When Polly repeated what she had said, both women began to cry inconsolably. In the short time he'd been with them, Dave had made a lasting impression on both women. That night, Polly and Peggy sat around drinking vodka and grieving together. Unfortunately, no amount of vodka could ease their pain.

In the morning, still in insurmountable pain, they had to make funeral arrangements for Dave's body. For the next couple of days Polly and Peggy went through the motions, renting rooms, cleaning rooms, and taking care of business. All the while they were both numb with grief.

Dave was laid to rest next to his brother Dale. It was a somber day for the family. In the days that followed Dave's burial, Peggy and Polly found it difficult to concentrate on their work. They drank in an effort to numb the grief they were both experiencing. With each day that passed, the pain began to subside.

CHAPTER 32

To her utter dismay, Polly was still having problems with Rick. He refused to stop calling her and making idle threats. She couldn't seem to make him understand that she didn't want to have anything more to do with him. When Rick called her for the umpteenth time, Polly told him to leave her alone, and he screamed, "Go screw yourself." After he hung up, Polly had the uneasy feeling that Rick was over the edge.

Polly's intuition about Rick's sanity was right. Having failed to convince Polly to take him back, Rick walked over to a drawer, pulled out a 38 revolver, and loaded it. He then got a piece of paper and wrote a short note saying that if he couldn't have Polly he didn't want to live. He looked in the mirror, and loathing what he saw, put the barrel of the revolver in his mouth and pulled the trigger.

The day after Rick shot himself, a friend called Polly to tell her that Rick had committed suicide. She told Polly that his mother had found him dead with the barrel of the revolver still in his mouth. Polly choked up as tears began streaming down her cheeks. She had once been very much in love with Rick but his drunkenness and unpredictable temper had destroyed their beautiful relationship. There was a part of her that still loved him, but there was no way she could have continued with such a tumultuous relationship. Rick's physical abuse had caused her to fear for her life, and Polly refused to live that way.

Polly now had one more friend to bury. For the fourth time, she would be burying a man she loved. It greatly saddened her. The motel was doing really well, but her personal life was in complete chaos.

Buying the motel had proven to be a very successful investment for Polly. She was making more money than she had anticipated. If her success in the motel business continued, Polly had no doubt that she could one day be a multimillionaire. After her grief over Rick's death subsided, Polly concentrated on the running of the motel. It was a lot more work than either Polly or Peggy had realized. The key to Polly's success as a motel owner was that she didn't mind hard work and she loved meeting new people. Truck drivers would rent rooms because the rates were quite reasonable. The fact that her daughters were living in Las Cruces made life easier for Polly. She loved being able to see her favorite grandson Toby whenever she wanted. Being a typical grandmother, Polly spoiled Toby the same way her own grandmother had spoiled her. He spent a lot of time with her while Judie, her daughter, was at work. Her family christened her motel "Pollywood" because, as far as they were concerned, Polly was rich, and she knew so many people.

Polly had bought Patti and Judie a mobile home so they had a roof over their heads. Also, she always made sure they had plenty of food because she never wanted them to go hungry. Judie met a guy named Tim, and they fell instantly in love. Tim liked Judie's son Toby, and little Toby had taken an instant liking to Tim. Tim was in the Army and stationed at White Sands. He asked Judie to marry him, and she accepted. When Tim was sent to Germany, he took his new family with him. At her first opportunity, Polly flew to Germany to visit Judie, Toby, and her new granddaughter Samantha. Judie was overjoyed by her mother's visit because she missed being around family.

During one of Polly's trips to Germany, Peggy met Mike. She fell in love and told Polly that she was going to move to Colorado with Mike. Polly tried to dissuade her, to no avail. Peggy was in love and wouldn't listen to reason. Polly didn't like Mike. He was a creep, just like Rick had been. Polly hadn't listened to Peggy when she tried to warn her about Rick, and now Peggy wouldn't listen to Polly's warning about Mike. Despite Peggy's move to Colorado, she and Polly would remain best friends forever.

After Peggy left, Polly felt very much alone without her best friend around. The two women had been together for over ten years. Peggy had been an enormous help to Polly with the motel. Although Peggy called Polly once in a while, Polly missed seeing her. Peggy had been Polly's confidante and was never critical or judgmental. Polly really missed that.

Finding herself so completely alone, Polly stayed up late at night contemplating how quickly time was passing. The thought depressed her. Running the motel was more work than Polly cared to do but she was making good money.

In the days that followed, Polly met lots of people. She also met some decent men with whom she would go to the bar and play pool. But playing pool and getting drunk was getting old. Polly fell into a state of depression.

Walt called to see how she was doing, and she told him she was doing very well. Hearing the tension in her voice, he suggested that she have some stress tests done. Polly took Walt's advice and scheduled an appointment with her doctor. The doctor put her on all kinds of medications. He had her on sleeping pills and tranquilizers. Polly was at one of the lowest points in her life. Despite the fact that she had made a lot of money with the motel, there was still something missing. Her life had become routine and she was terribly unhappy. Polly fell into an even greater state of depression.

One day she met a man named Matt. Matt was a very nice retired Navy man who had lost his wife and was living in Polly's RV Park. His great love was guns. Polly never considered him sexually attractive, but he was a kind and gentle soul with a big heart. When Polly's work day ended, she and Matt would spend a couple of hours playing cards. Since Peggy was no longer around, she got close to Matt. He was good to her, and for the first time in her life it was not a sexual relationship. He was a good friend with whom she could converse. She and Matt would spend hours just talking.

Polly continued to take her medication because she was stressed about many things in her life and the pills calmed her nerves. It was a good thing she had reliable employees to help her run the motel because the work was never-ending. People from every part of the country came and went. Almost every room was being rented. Polly was getting tired and needed a vacation.

When Judie, Tim, Toby, and Samantha returned from Germany, Polly offered Judie and Tim the job of managing the motel. They needed a job and a place to stay. It would be the perfect arrangement because Polly needed a vacation. With a long vacation in mind, Polly bought a new motor home.

At Judie's suggestion, Polly and Matt loaded up the motor home and headed out. Polly had never been so glad to get away. She and Matt decided to head for California to visit some of her classmates from Pipestone, Minnesota. She hadn't seen them since their last high school reunion.

After a few days on the road, Polly was feeling a whole lot better, but she continued taking her medications as a safety precaution. She had been to California several times with Walt when he had flown some dignitaries to Los Angeles. Polly had always found the West Coast exciting and fast-paced. What she really liked about the West Coast was the weather – it was always nice. She and Walt would spend hours walking barefoot on the beach. They had visited all the tourist spots as well as the movie stars' homes in Hollywood. There was so much to do in California.

Polly and Matt traveled up the Coast to San Francisco. She was becoming very fond of Matt. He was a lot of fun to be with. Since he loved guns, they attended shooting events all over California. They were having a great time, and Polly didn't want to return to Las Cruces and all the problems she had left behind. Things weren't the same now that Peggy was gone. The grief of losing four people she loved had taken its toll on her. This vacation had been great therapy for her. The vacation ended all too soon. When it was time for Polly and Matt to return to Las Cruces, Polly really didn't want to.

A week after her return to Las Cruces, Polly was faced with a problem she had to resolve. She and Tim didn't see eye to eye on a lot of things. The motel business was one of them. Polly offered Tim and Judie $10,000 if they vacated their position as managers. They agreed, and Polly got her motel back to run as she saw fit. The situation upset Judie and created some animosity between mother and daughter. Polly felt she had invested too much work, time, and money to let it all fall apart.

The six weeks Polly and Matt spent in California had been a godsend. Now that she was back, she was faced with new problems added to old ones. A permanent vacation might just be the way to go. Or she could retire and live on a beach for the rest of her life. Unfortunately it would have to wait. The mortgage payments had to be made. She was finally beginning to make a profit, which she invested. Some of her investments were good, while others were not so good. Polly invested some of her money in IRAs and stocks. She was making more money than she knew what to do with. She made large loans to her children, but they had to pay her back with interest. For Christmas, Polly would buy her grandchildren only the very best. Things were finally on track for Polly. Her grandchildren loved going to "Pollywood" to visit grandma and swim in her big swimming pool.

Polly's luck changed for the better. She had found a good friend in Matt. They would play cards every day. They talked, laughed, and had a great time together. Polly cherished these precious moments in her life.

Polly had always wanted to go on a Love Boat Cruise, so she called a travel agency to make the arrangements. It was still winter and she didn't want to take the cruise till spring.

One night out of the blue, Polly received a phone call from Peggy. She was calling from New York City where she and Mike had moved from Colorado. Peggy and Mike weren't getting along, and she asked Polly if she could have her old job back. Polly told her she could have it back any time she wanted it. Peggy caught the first flight out of New York City and headed back to Las Cruces. Peggy now realized she had made a big mistake. Polly had tried to warn her but Peggy was so much in love she wouldn't listen.

When Peggy arrived in El Paso, Polly was waiting for her. They were so glad to see each other again they began to cry. The first thing they did was go to the airport bar and order a drink. Polly wanted to know everything Peggy had been up to since she left Las Cruces. She told Peggy how very much she had missed her and made her promise never to leave again, which Peggy did. The two women had always had a good time together, and now was no different. They didn't care who was watching because when they were together, no one else existed.

When they arrived at the motel, Peggy said she hadn't realized how much she had missed it. She and Polly stayed up half the night catching up on old times. They laughed till they were both crying.

In the morning, Polly and Peggy were up at the crack of dawn drinking coffee and enjoying each other's company. They had missed each other more than either one of them cared to admit. They had been through a lot together. Polly told Peggy about the cruise she was planning in the spring. Peggy told Polly she would take care of the motel in her absence, so Polly called the travel agency to verify the arrangements. She told Peggy that this cruise was long over-due. All she had ever done was work, work, work. She felt it was time to slow down, enjoy some time off and spend some of the money she had worked so hard to accumulate.

On weekends, Peggy and Polly went shopping at the mall. They found some beautiful evening gowns that Polly could take on her cruise. She had always loved buying only the most fashionable clothes that money could buy. Now she could afford it.

CHAPTER 33

In late May she flew to Los Angeles, California where she would board the cruise ship that would sail along the California and Mexican coast. When she arrived in California, Polly took a cab to a hotel near the docks where she rented a room. She was so excited! She had never been on a cruise before. Her dream was finally becoming a reality. Polly was feeling a lot better about herself and the fact that things would improve. She was beginning to climb out of her rut. Her business was doing really well, and she was ready to enjoy her life.

After she checked into a room she freshened up and ordered room service. It was a simple lunch, which she ate while she watched television. When she finished eating, she decided to take a nap because she was suffering from jet lag. Polly lay on the bed and closed her eyes. She thought about Matt, and having been with so many men, she wondered if he was the right man for her. At least he didn't treat her like a sex object. Matt respected her as a person and she liked that. But there was a part of her that was still searching for a knight in shining armor.

The following morning, Polly was up early and had breakfast in the hotel restaurant. By 10:00 a.m. she was at the docks ready to board the cruise ship. She had never seen a Love Boat cruise ship before and found it to be quite impressive. It was much larger than it appeared on television commercials. Passengers arrived and began boarding the ship. It was a beautiful day for a cruise.

Once everyone was on board, the Love Boat pulled up anchor. Many people lined the deck waving to their loved ones as the ship began its journey. The soft ocean breeze kissed Polly's face. The ship sailed farther and farther away from the docks until all Polly could see was water. The salty sea air was exhilarating, and Polly felt a contentment she hadn't experienced in a long time.

Polly was surrounded by conversation and laughter. Since she had never been on a ship before, Polly prayed she wouldn't get seasick. She took the elevator down to the main lobby and found it to be magnificent. There were a lot of people walking around. The purser accompanied Polly to her quarters. Upon entering her room, she was amazed at how beautifully it was designed. Everything was in its place and she felt right at home. As the ship silently sailed through the water, Polly walked over to a stereo that was built into the wall. After she turned it on, she sat on the bed listening to the soft, soothing music. She was afraid to close her eyes, fearing that when she opened them again, she would discover she had only been dreaming. Polly could hear people talking in the hallway who seemed just as content as she was.

All the years of hard work had finally paid off. This is what she had worked so hard for. Now she could enjoy life without worrying about finances.

Later that evening, Polly dressed in one of the elegant evening gowns she had brought with her. As she made her way to the dining room, men stared. Polly looked stunning! The admiring stares of the older men as she made her entrance made her feel beautiful.

The maitre d' quickly ushered Polly to a table. Even though the place was filled with handsome people, Polly knew all eyes were on her. These were the kinds of moments Polly lived for. She had never been shy. Polly was a people person. It wouldn't take her long to mix right in. They all seemed really nice.

A very handsome man with white hair stared at Polly all through dinner. Having finished her dinner, she walked into the lounge where a live band was performing. Polly walked to a corner of the bar away from the crowd where she would be less conspicuous. There were mirrors everywhere, which made the place look larger than it really was. Polly sat at a booth where she could see everyone who walked in. The air was filled with music and laughter. The band was playing 50's music. An adorable young waitress approached her and asked if she would like something to drink. Polly ordered a Tequila Sunrise. The waitress looked like she was twenty-five years old, with long blonde hair that hung past her waist. She had a nice figure and a dazzling smile. As she walked away, Polly recalled her younger days when she was busy being a housewife and raising kids. There was never any time for a vacation. If it were possible to do it all again, she would do it differently.

The waitress brought her drink and Polly took a sip. It tasted delicious. The lounge began to get crowded, and before too long everyone started to get inebriated. The place got really noisy with loud chatter and music. A dignified-looking gentleman had been eyeing Polly as she walked down the stairs on her way to the lounge. At his first opportunity, he walked to where she was sitting and asked her to dance. She accepted, and as they walked to the dance floor he held her hand. His touch made her tremble. As it turned out, he was a very good dancer. After a few dances Polly decided to call it a night. She was feeling rather tipsy. Polly was no longer the young girl who could party all night. Besides, she wanted to get up early so she could see the Mexican coast. She loved gazing out at the ocean.

The cruise lasted only three days, and much too soon she found herself back in Las Cruces. Polly vowed to take a longer cruise the next time since she now had the freedom and the money to go anywhere she chose. Where she had once struggled, she was now a self-made millionaire. She was living in "Pollywood" and owned the only motel on Motel Boulevard. This made her the Queen of Motel Boulevard.

On November 7, 1999 Polly made the last payment on her loan. The motel, RV park, and restaurant were now all hers. It had been a long haul, but Polly paid back her entire loan just as she had promised. Her determination not to give up despite the many obstacles she had encountered made it possible for Polly to fulfill her dreams. She loved Las Cruces so much that it was where she wanted to spend the rest of her life.

Even though Polly had been boy crazy all her life and had struggled through many difficult and sometimes harrowing times, hers is a story of success.

Throughout the course of her life she has kept in touch with her classmates. They still communicate with each other as often as possible. Polly attended her 50th Class Reunion, at which she and her classmates had a fabulous time.

Las Cruces has become Polly's home, but Pipestone will always remain dear to her heart.

THE END

Jay Dee Ruybal lives in Santa Fe, New Mexico
with his wife and two children. Ruybal's first
book, his autobiographical THE DRUG HAZED
WAR IN SOUTHEAST ASIA, has received
favorable reviews. His next book will be
released later this year.